SEVEN FACES OF LOVE

SEVEN FACES OF *L*OVE

by

ANDRÉ MAUROIS

TRANSLATED BY HAAKON M. CHEVALIER

DIDIER

New York

"When one does not love too much,
one does not love enough."

Pascal

SEVEN FACES
OF LOVE

SEVEN FACES OF LOVE

CHIVALROUS LOVE

The Princess of Clèves

*T*HE RELATION between feeling and literature is like the relation between government and public opinion. The strength of government depends, in the last analysis, on public opinion, but public opinion is itself created or vitiated by government. Thus feeling inspires literature, and literature in turn transforms and at times creates feeling.

Sexual desire, which is the source of the feeling of love, remains a virtually unchanging instinct; it varies as little as human bodies; but the manifestations of this instinct, which are the ways of loving, become modified in the course of centuries. Can two more different senti-

3

ments be imagined than Chloë's voluptuous love for Daphnis, and Mme de Mortsauf's chaste love for Félix de Vandenesse? Than the simple and naive love of the Chevalier des Grieux for Manon Lescaut and the intellectual love of one of Aldous Huxley's heroes? The same desires, according to the times and philosophies, produce prodigiously diverse reactions.

The present work proposes to deal with several variations in the sentiment of love in the course of three centuries of French literature.

1. *THE BIRTH OF ROMANTIC LOVE*

The Ancients did not, like ourselves, make the passions of love the essential theme of their fiction. The Homeric hero went into a fury if someone abducted his captive, but this was due to pride rather than jealousy. The beauty of Helen caused the outbreak of the War of Troy, but in the *Iliad* Helen's sentiments play only a small role. Penelope was a virtuous spouse; she was not a lover. All love that went beyond desire was regarded as madness. Plato alone among the Greeks of the classic period speaks of a love so intense that it demands purity. Among the Romans adultery flourished, but it was a crime, not a drama. Virgil, Catullus, Tibullus, Proper-

4

tius, had some presentiment of our torments, but Ovid's *Art of Love* was only a manual of cynicism.

Not before the twelfth and the thirteenth centuries of our era, the time of the *troubadours* and the *trouvères*, do we discover, first in the poetic courts of love, then in the romances of chivalry, something that resembles the complex sentiments that Pascal calls the *Passions of Love*. Why, at about that time, did so much importance come to be attached to the sentimental and spiritual reactions that accompanied desire? First, because Christianity had given woman an altogether different status from the one she occupied before it. By imposing on woman the constraint of modesty, by multiplying moral obstacles around her, it involuntarily augmented the intensity of the passions she aroused.

But, it will be said, the matrons of the Roman republic were not lacking in modesty.

This is true, but marriage among the Ancients, being a utilitarian contract, which in no sense obliged the man to be faithful, did not create inner conflicts in him; Christian marriage, being much more exacting, was also much more difficult for violent and still half-pagan creatures to submit to—whence constraint, anguish and passion.

It may also be objected that Chivalry existed long before the romances of chivalry.

5

For romantic love to be born Christianity had indeed to blend with other currents. In the South of France, the land of the courts of love, whence Dante and Petrarch derived the traditions of courtly love, these other currents were an Arab poetry wholly impregnated with Platonism, the ardent language of the heroines of Virgil and Ovid, and also (as Denis de Rougement suggests) the heretical Christianity of the Catharians, which taught total chastity. In this sect bonds were developed between men and women that had no touch of the carnal.

But, it will be asked, were not most of the romances of chivalry written further north and even in England?

The poetry of the troubadours was known further north, having penetrated first into the court of France, then into that of England, through Queen Eleanor of Aquitania. It fused wonderfully with another, the Celtic tradition. The Celts, a dreamy and passionate race, had brought to occidental Europe a sense of mystery, a constant meditation on death, which are not Mediterranean. Their brooding, their reveries, were propitious to the birth of sentiments more complex than desire. The romance of Tristan and Yseult contains the essence of the Celtic conception of love. In it desire becomes passion, and frustrated passion finds refuge only in death.

Finally, as Albert Thibaudet saw very clearly, the romance of love developed about the time of the Crusades

6

because at that time it found a public, and even two publics. It appealed to the public of the pilgrims, very numerous at a time when everyone yearned to go to Jerusalem, to Saint-Jacques de Compostelle, to Rome. The traveler who is far away from a woman imagines her more desirable and more perfect. Deprived of the society of women, the pilgrims took pleasure in reading tales whose unreal and sublime heroines peopled their dreams. And the romances also had a second public, which was that of the women, who in the Middle Ages occupied an eminent place in society and received an education about equal to that of men.

In the absence of the warrior, so often kept in foreign lands by the Crusade or by feudal war, the men who remained at the château were pages, almost children, who dared to love the lady only with respect. She was the Mistress in more than one sense. To the women the Romances of the Round Table promised an extraordinary change in their destinies. They suddenly became more interesting and more complex personages. They saw themselves no longer merely desired, but courted. Thanks to the support of the romances, they could impose on men the respect of constant love which is not a natural sentiment in man. Women wished men to be Lancelot or Tristan. This did not prevent them from yielding to Don Juan who, by making them suffer, filled their lives,

7

but it was only in order to come back to Lancelot who would protect them against themselves and who would sacrifice his own happiness to make them forget Don Juan. The romances of chivalry surrounded them with a whole world of Lancelots; it was a climate in which they thrived.

The creation, through the romance of chivalry, of the romantic hero in real life is all the more remarkable since the men who were thus transformed were warriors, of a violent, often despotic nature, who must at the beginning have found it humiliating to respect the caprices and demands of a woman. It is very remarkable to find, in Froissart, that a sovereign like Edward the Third of England, a man who was very brutal in his methods of government, could become, through the effect of the romances, a true lover in the seventeenth-century sense, gallant, timid, pining when he is separated from the woman he loves, not daring to force her consent—though she is alone and he is King. One feels that the powerful impact of literature has exerted itself on this primitive soul and has subjugated it.

All civilization is ceremony. There is no other way of overcoming the barbarism latent in the heart of man than to chain it with rules. This is what courtly love did. The trials and labors imposed on the man by the lady of his dreams, the jousts in which he participates before her eyes while wearing her colors, the songs that he composes for her, end by playing such a role in his life that physical desire is relegated to an inferior plane, and is even sometimes forgotten. Chivalry, in the Christian world, subjugated both love and war. The romance of chivalry and romantic love were powerful elements of civilization.

2. THE ECLIPSE AND THE REBIRTH OF THE ROMANTIC

Between the thirteenth and the seventeenth centuries, romantic love undergoes several eclipses.

a) As soon as there are found, in life itself, too great a number of heroes of romance, the taste for the romance declines. Courtesy becomes gallantry; gallantry gives rise to irony. Don Quixote becomes the just parody of the romances of chivalry. The transformation of Aldonza Lorenzo into Dulcinea is but the caricature of the transfiguration of every loved woman in the mind of her lover.

b) In order to have time to analyze sentiments, to speak of them, in order that the love conquest may be slow and studied, and thereby worthy of being narrated, it is necessary that the man and the woman meet at

9

leisure. A stable civilization must shelter men and give them time to love, that is to say, time to dream. Now the great civilization of the Middle Ages begins to break up as early as the fourteenth century. This is a period of humanity in which feudal civilization is already decadent, in which monarchic civilization is not yet perfected. It is a long epoch of violence, of disorder and of instability. The Hundred Years' War, the civil wars, the religious wars, leave little leisure to lovers. It is for many men a time of hurried, rather brutal loves; a time of lust rather than of love. Read Brantôme, Boccaccio, Rabelais, Chaucer.

During this eclipse of sentimentality, the romantic refuge of women is poetry, and more particularly the pastoral. From Virgil to Shakespeare, from Ronsard to Racan, from Rousseau to Tolstoy, human beings have always loved to imagine a bucolic golden age in which shepherds and shepherdesses, in a conventionalized and kindly natural setting, can give themselves over to idyllic passions. One need only have lived in the country to know that nature is on the contrary cruel and exacting, that the efficient tending of flocks is scarcely compatible with romantic adventures. But pastorals are written by city poets.

Finally at the beginning of the seventeenth century, under Henri IV, order returns to France. Sentiments and leisure are simultaneously reborn. After the Fronde rebellion, which is the last spurt of a dying feudalism, the seventeenth century witnesses the transformation of a warlike and political nobility into a nobility of the *salons*. The great individuals of the Renaissance are forced to accept the authority of the State, which is the King's. This is not accomplished without difficulty. We see, in the *Memoirs* of the Cardinal de Retz, what those men and women of the *Fronde* were like: La Rochefoucauld, Madame de Longueville, *la Grande Mademoiselle*, Lauzun . . .

They are great and handsome human animals, difficult to domesticate, and in many ways resemble the people of the Renaissance. "All that the nobility is good for," says the Duke of Saint-Simon in his *Memoirs*, "is to get itself killed." During the minority of Louis XIV, four thousand nobles perished in duels; between 1549 and 1607, seven thousand. When, to bring back order into the country, the King is obliged to forbid them to settle their private quarrels at the head of armed troops, when he shuts them up in a court, in *salons* which are like cages to them, they shake the bars till they break, whence the necessity of imposing forms upon them, and even an excess of forms, which becomes preciosity. "All is intricate politeness in gestures and in words, all is naive ferocity in morals."

There is no greater error than to imagine the great classics as insensitive beings, simply because in their works the passions assume the mask of Alexandrine verses and of tragedies imitated from the Ancients. There is an excellent book on this subject by Fidao-Justiniani entitled *What is a Classic?* Fidao-Justiniani shows that the ideal of the men of the seventeenth century was by no means coldness, but greatness. In *The Princess of Clèves* the word *great* recurs on every page. In the tragedies too, "The great heart that shines forth in the words that you speak . . ." The people of this time are thirsty for glory, and strength of passions appears to them a title to glory. "I am tender to the point of madness," says Madame de Sévigné. They all believe that a *generous* being, that is, one of good birth, must love with fury.

Everyone at the time wept with extraordinary facility. There is constant reference to streams, to torrents of tears. When Turenne dies all the passers-by weep in the streets. And it is true that the greatest of our writers, Racine, Madame de La Fayette, give to these furies modest expressions and restrained movements; but this moderation, this modesty, are all the more beautiful by virtue of the fact that they dominate stronger passions. A great classic work is a hurricane, a chaos of sentiments reduced to order. It is because the passions which a Racine or a Madame de La Fayette express are ardent that the marvelous order of the constructions in which they are set astonishes and delights us.

Toward the middle of the seventeenth century there live in Paris a race of strong and violent beings upon whom a mode of existence has been imposed which no longer allows their passions to be liberated by action. What do these untamed captives read? They seek in books a representation of the great actions and the great emotions that life now refuses them. Once again the romances of chivalry come into fashion. Madame de Sévigné herself, for all her reasonableness, reads *The Great Cyrus.* "The beauty of the sentiments," she says, "the violence of the passions, the greatness of the events and the miraculous successes of their formidable swords, all this carries me away as though I were a little girl."

All Europe dotes on Honoré d'Urfé's *L'Astrée*, a pastoral of five thousand pages, extremely well written, longer than all the novels of Marcel Proust and which the Frenchmen of the time knew by heart, as the Puritans knew their Bible. *L'Astrée* taught the omnipotence of woman and painted in Céladon the model of lovers. The laws of Céladon were those of romantic love:

(1) *One must love to excess.*
(2) *Have no other passion but one's love.*

(3) *Love one woman only.*

(4) *Have the sole ambition to please the woman one loves.*

(5) *Defend one's shepherdess.*

(6) *Find her perfect in every way.*

(7) *Have no other will but hers.*

(8) *Promise to love her always.*

A whole society lived thus. They wanted to do "great" things, but to do great things "for their shepherdess," for the loved woman. "Return victorious from a combat whose prize is Chimène . . ." The most illustrious, the most wise, have a tendency to make love a duty. "Passion," says Pascal in his *Discourse on the Passions of Love,* "cannot be beautiful without excess. When one does not love too much, one does not love enough." There is sanctity in this conception of love. One sacrifices everything to it, one grows sick with it, one even dies of it and is proud of dying of it. In short the heroic ideal, unable to express itself any longer through deeds of war, has sought refuge in love. Sublime sentiments, but having their full value only on condition of remaining rather rare. That a Pascal could have loved thus, or a La Rochefoucauld in his youth, we are willing to accept. If the violence of passion becomes a rule, such a claim verges on the comical.

14

This love that takes up one's whole life soon becomes merely a game. People take to exploring *La Carte du Tendre*. They "de-labyrinth their sentiments." A factitious sensibility replaces natural desires. It was of the young Chevalier de Sévigné that it was said, "His whole ambition was to die of a love which he did not feel . . ." Devotion to a mistress had been admirable at a time when it inspired great actions; but love, if it engages the whole man, quickly becomes anti-social. Immediately comedy, a social chastisement, reacts. Molière ridicules the extravagances of the *Précieuses*. Boileau accuses Mademoiselle de Scudéry of having dressed up all the bourgeois of her district as heroes. La Rochefoucauld analyses passions to find in them a residue of self-love. Under the influence of these great realists, taste is purified. The romantic ideal is attacked by a mocking bourgeoisie and by the *"honnête homme"* who has no pretensions, not even that of loving more than he loves. Women weary of Céladon and of a love that is too respectful. "Ah! Why does he not become a little bolder? . . ." A stoic reaction announces the birth of the best classicism, and it was only in the following century that the excesses of the kind of subtle love-play that came to be known as *marivaudage* led to those of licentiousness.

But before disappearing, the heroic ideal, applied to the passions of love, was to produce its masterpiece which is *The Princess of Clèves.* This novel is a kind of miracle because it maintains a perfect equilibrium between the vigor of the passions and the moderation of its tone. To the long crisis of romantic love which we have just described French civilization owes one of its most precious attributes, which is the art of analyzing sentiments. If no other language can paint with as delightful exactness as the French the most delicate shades of love, if amorous conversation has become in France the most charming and the most perfect of arts, we owe it in part to the *Précieuses* and even to Mademoiselle de Scudéry, in part to the great moralists, and in part also to Racine; but we also owe it to the woman, so keen, so wise, and so modest, who succeeded, without irony and without excess, in bringing the novel back to the plane of reality and who showed that the beauty of the most ardent sentiments can be painted in the simplest language: I am referring to Madame de La Fayette.

3. *THE AUTHOR*

Madame de La Lafayette's maiden name was Marie-Madeleine de La Vergne. Her mother, early widowed, had become married again to a Chevalier Renaud de Sévigné, so that the two most remarkable women of the

seventeenth century came to be related. Mademoiselle
de la Vergne had received the excellent education of girls
of that time. Like Madame de Sévigne, she had had the
erudite poet Ménage for a teacher. Poor Ménage had
loved all his life and although on reaching the age of fifty
he had considered it necessary to make a round of visits to
his fair ones, to inform them that he was giving up love,
he still liked to have it believed that an amorous friendship prevailed between his pupils and himself. A quat-
rain in circulation at the time runs as follows:

> Forget the marquise and the countess;
> Ménage, your conceit is sublime.
> Instead of winning their bounties,
> You will only be wasting your time.

> *Laissez-là comtesse et marquise;*
> *Ménage, vous n'êtes pas fin.*
> *Au lieu d'y gagner leur franchise,*
> *Vous y perdrez votre latin.*

But far from wasting his time Ménage succeeded in
teaching Latin to Marie-Madeleine de La Vergne, who,
no doubt, owed the firmness of her style to this.

Mademoiselle de La Vergne was introduced to society
shortly after the Fronde. Which is to say that she had a
very free youth. Bussy, the malicious gossip, drew up a

map on which the names of women were substituted for the names of towns, which enabled him to recount metaphorically the assaults made upon these places and to name the besiegers. "La Vergne," says this map, "is a very pretty town and so devout that the Archbishop has dwelt there with the Duc de Brissac, who since the prelate's departure has remained its chief governor." The Archbishop is none other than the Cardinal de Retz, but the latter himself confesses in his *Memoirs* that although he paid assiduous court to the lovable La Vergne, it was without success.

In spite of her grace and her intelligence, Mademoiselle de La Vergne at twenty-two was not yet married, which was uncommon at the time. She therefore resigned herself to making an "arranged" marriage with a Count de La Fayette, a man of high birth and of little wit who, at their first meeting, found precisely nothing to say to this too brilliant girl. The song-writers composed some lines on this subject:

The fair one when questioned on her husband-to-be
Said to her friends, "He seems extremely sweet to me,
    Quite decent and upright,
    Though not so very bright!
But, all things considered, it will be quite a catch
    If I make such a match."

La Belle, consultée sur son futur époux,
Dit dans cette assemblée qu'il paraissait fort doux
  Et d'un air fort honnête
  Quoique peut-être bête!
Mais qu'après tout, pour elle, un tel mari
  Etait un bon parti.

A few years ago a publisher brought out a collection of *Lives* of so-called *Obscure Husbands and Wives,* in which Monsieur de Staël and Madame de Chateaubriand figured. It would have been natural to include a work devoted to Monsieur de La Fayette. Monsieur de La Fayette is even more than an obscure husband, he is a non-existent husband. The Comte d'Haussonville, in his book on Madame de La Fayette, quotes in connection with Monsieur de La Fayette this passage from La Bruyère: "There are women who obliterate or bury their husbands to the point where no mention is made of them in society. 'Is he still living? Is he not living?' One doubts it. His only function in the family is to serve as an example of timid silence and of perfect submission. He is entitled neither to a dowry nor to articles of deed, but aside from this and the fact that he does not bear children, he is the woman, she is the husband."

Between Monsieur and Madame de La Fayette there were no disagreements. He adored her. She "loved him very much," that is to say not at all. She soon left him to return to Paris; he lived in the country. Monsieur d'Haussonville has proved that he died only in 1683, so that Madame de La Fayette was married twenty-eight years. No one had been aware of it, not even she.

In Paris, Madame de La Fayette became the most intimate friend of the delightful Henriette d'Angleterre, *Madame,* the sister-in-law of Louis XIV. In memory of *Madame* she was for a long time on an excellent footing with the King, but she had retired from the court after her friend's death and thenceforth lived only for a few intimate friends.

These friends were not numerous. Madame de La Fayette did not wish a brilliant *salon.* She disliked all display. She had been nicknamed *Le Brouillard* (the fog), and one readily visualizes her in a sentimental haze. She was romantic and dreamy. She was almost always suffering from fever, which never became higher. In no circumstance did Madame de La Fayette show bitterness or anger. True, authentic, sure, in her semi-retirement she wrote novels which she did not even sign. She was a great writer and did not want it to be known, an excellent Latinist who never spoke of her Latin, a tender and faithful friend who did not parade her friendships. But these were of quality. She had kept her old master, Ménage; she received Segré and Huet; Madame de

Sévigné loved Madame de La Fayette almost as much as she loved her daughter, Madame de Grignan, as a consequence of which Madame de Grignan did not care much for Madame de La Fayette. And above all there was Monsieur de La Rochefoucauld.

The Duc de La Rochefoucauld had had the most romantic life, for which he was not cut out. Retz has depicted him admirably: "There has always been something mysterious about Monsieur de La Rochefoucauld. He was ambitious to be mixed up in political intrigues from the time of his childhood; at a time when he was not attracted to the ordinary pursuits of private life (to which he has never been addicted), and had no knowledge of affairs of state (which, on the other hand, have never been his strong point). He was never a man of business, and I do not know why; for he had gifts which in any other man would have supplied the place of those he lacked."

He had been the lover of those Amazons, the Duchesse de Chevreuse and the Duchesse de Longueville. At the age of twenty-four, while he was still the Prince de Marcillac, he had formed the fine project of abducting Queen Anne of Austria and one of her maids of honor, Mademoiselle de Hautefort from under the very noses of the King, Louis XIII, and the Cardinal de Richelieu. Then Madame de Longueville had dragged him into the follies of the Fronde, where he received a bullet-wound that nearly robbed him of his sight. It was then that he caused a portrait of Madame de Longueville to be engraved with these verses:

Waging war on the King, I have lost both my eyes,
But I could have stormed the Heavens for such a prize.

Faisant la guerre au Roi, j'ai perdu les deux yeux,
Mais, pour un tel objet, je l'aurais faite aux Dieux.

A little later, having learned of Madame de Longueville's unfaithfulness, he corrected his couplet:

For an inconstant heart that I now could despise
I waged war on the King; I thereby lost my eyes.

Pour un coeur inconstant qu'enfin je connais mieux
J'ai fait la guerre au Roi; j'en ai perdu les yeux.

He was surely thinking of Madame de Longueville when he wrote this maxim: "When our love grows cold, we are well content to meet with unfaithfulness so as to obtain release from our own vows."

After the amnesty, having grown melancholy and disillusioned, he is for a long time a voluntary exile in his Château of Verteuil. This Don Juan now keeps his face all bundled up and wears dark glasses over his ailing eyes.

Finally at Mazarin's death he decides to return to Paris, and reopens his mansion, the Hôtel de Liancourt, on Rue de Seine. He was now forty-eight years old. He had a gift for writing and he did not lack violent passions to express. It was the period of literary games and pastimes. At Madame de Scudéry's they wrote madrigals; at Madame de Sablé's, maxims. La Rochefoucauld composed some extremely disenchanted ones. Life had disappointed him. Women had used his love to compromise him in their intrigues. He considers that true love is like the apparition of spirits: "Everyone speaks of it and few people have seen it . . ." that "Virtue in woman is often the result of love of her reputation and ease" and that "Judged by most of its effects, love is more like hate than friendship." In short he is, like Byron, cynical through disillusion and undoubtedly romantic at heart like Byron.

Was La Rochefoucauld the friend or the lover of Madame de La Fayette? This is a very controversial question. When she met him he was close to fifty; which is not for everyone the age of retirement. The dangerous Bussy questions Mademoiselle de Scudéry on the subject. This is what she answers: "Monsieur de La Rochefoucauld's relations with Madame de La Fayette are quite honorable. There is nothing to indicate that they go beyond friendship. Most likely the fear of God on both sides, and perhaps politics, have clipped love's wings.

She is his favorite and his greatest friend." As for La Rochefoucauld himself, he writes at about the same time: "As for light amours, I have in the past indulged in these to some extent; but now I do so no longer in spite of my youth. I have given up pretty compliments, and can only wonder that there are still so many men of honor who spend their time in peddling them . . ."

But, again like Byron, he was one of those men who proudly say, "No attachments," and ask only to be attached. It is a fact that he spent all the end of his life with Madame de La Fayette. Each day he would leave his mansion on Rue de Seine to pay her a visit, at her mansion on Rue Férou, at the corner of Rue de Vaugirard. This mansion had a garden with a fountain and a little arbor, of which Madame de Sévigné said that it was the prettiest spot in Paris for the spirit to bask in. How many times, on beautiful summer evenings, La Rochefoucauld, Madame de Sévigné and Madame de La Fayette would remain chatting far into the night, either in the garden or around Madame de La Fayette's gold-laced bed!

When this friendship began, many of La Rochefoucauld's *Maxims* were already written. It was not through him that Madame de La Fayette had come to know them and she had been appalled by their pessimism. "What corruption there must be in the mind and heart of one capable of thinking up such things!"

There still exists a copy of the *Maxims* annotated by Madame de La Fayette. Sainte-Beuve has described it for us. It enables us to see the gentle and beneficent influence she exerted on La Rochefoucauld, whose pessimism she tends to soften. Often she writes in the margin, "True . . . Excellent . . . Sublime . . ." But sometimes she criticizes and ridicules a certain preciosity in which La Rochefoucauld indulges. When La Rochefoucauld says, "The only cause for astonishment is one's perpetual capacity for astonishment," Madame de La Fayette writes in the margin, "rubbish." Or sometimes again, "Pretentious nonsense . . . Trite . . . Commonplace . . . This is true, but not always . . ." When she reads, "What men have named friendship is merely a transaction from which self-love always expects to reap some gain," she writes, "This goes for common friendship, but not for the true." When the maxim says, "Love may be rare, but true friendship is rarer still," Madame de La Fayette answers, "I believe both to be equally rare, for the true quality of friendship has an element of love, and the true quality of love has also an element of friendship." Sometimes she comments without prudishness on a maxim on women. La Rochefoucauld had written, "The reason why women are not usually very susceptible to friendship is that they find it insipid after they have experienced love," Madame de La Fayette answers, "This is because love encompasses everything—mind, heart, and body." Finally, in the margin of this maxim, "Marriage sometimes brings content, but never bliss," she answers, "I do not know if it brings bliss, but I believe it may."

It seems that she could say with good reason, "Monsieur de La Rochefoucauld has given me wit, but I have reformed his heart." One likes to imagine this sweet and gentle little woman by the side of the great nobleman, somewhat somber, with his afflicted eyes, his fretful expression. With her mists she envelops the summit of that still rumbling volcano. As a game they set themselves to composing novels together. Mademoiselle de Scudéry says to Bussy,

"Monsieur de La Rochefoucauld and Madame de La Fayette have done a novel, which is said to be admirably well written. They are past the age of doing other things together."

"I should be sorry," Bussy answers, "were these authors younger, for they would amuse themselves by doing other things together, which would not be so entertaining for us as their book."

They think of their past. La Rochefoucauld evokes the loves of the Prince de Marcillac; Madame de La Fayette remembers the flirtations of Mademoiselle de La Vergne.

26

"Thus these two souls grown old would go back in imagination to that lovely springtime of their lives when they had not known each other and could not have loved each other." And thus was born *The Princess of Clèves*, whose heroine has something of Madame de La Fayette's modesty and whose hero, Monsieur de Nemours, recalls La Rochefoucauld as a young man.

4. THE BOOK

The Princess of Clèves takes place at the court of France, at the court of Henri II. Mademoiselle de Chartres, ravishing and perfect in every way, marries the Prince de Clèves. It is a marriage of reason. Mademoiselle de Chartres has the greatest esteem for her future husband. She does not love him, but she does not know love; she marries in perfectly good faith and with the firm intention to be faithful. By misfortune and by chance, the Princesse de Clèves meets at a ball Monsieur de Nemours, who is the most seductive gentleman at the court and the flower of French chivalry. She loves him first without being willing to admit it to herself. Then jealousy reveals her own feelings to her. She is disturbed, ashamed, and finally decides to confide in her husband. She believes at first that so much frankness inspires gratitude, but such gratitude soon becomes jealousy. For Monsieur de Clèves it is a frightful torture to think that his wife loves another, and that this other man is so attractive. In the end Monsieur de Clèves dies, since in the seventeenth century people die of love. Now Madame de Clèves is free and one might think she is going to marry Nemours, but not at all. She rejects him because she thinks that Nemours and she are responsible for Monsieur de Clèves' death. But she continues to love him. Soon she herself dies of melancholy, after having spent her last days in austerity and devotion.

Such is the subject and we see at once that it deals with the theme of heroic love. We are here in the sector of *Tristan* and not in that of *Dangerous Relations*. Let us now look at details.

Mademoiselle de Chartres has the most exalted idea of the virtue and the duties of a woman. She has been brought up by a mother who would often paint her pictures of love, who would show her "what was agreeable in it, the better to persuade her of its dangers, which she taught her. She told her of men's insincerity, their deceit and their faithlessness, the domestic calamities caused by illicit love-affairs; on the other hand, the calm that reigned in the life of a faithful wife, and how virtue gives distinction and dignity to one who has rank and beauty."

This is a eulogy of virtue founded on its useful effects rather than on our duties.

Monsieur de Clèves is no less praiseworthy; he is a man deserving to be loved, and his wife believes she loves him. But he himself has too much experience not to know that she loves him not at all.

"Monsieur de Clèves, after his marriage, was happy, without, however, being entirely satisfied. He was distressed to see that the feelings of Mademoiselle de Chartres did not go beyond esteem and gratitude, and he could not flatter himself that she might be hiding more gratifying ones, since their relationship permitted her to show them without shocking her extreme modesty. Scarcely a day passed but he complained to her of this.

" 'Is it possible,' he would say to her, 'that I can be other than happy in marrying you? Yet 'tis true that I am not happy. You feel for me only a sort of kindness that cannot satisfy me. You are neither impatient, nor uneasy, nor fretful; you are no more touched by my passion than you would be by an attachment founded merely on the advantage of your fortune, and not on your personal charms.'

" 'Your complaint is unjust,' she answered. 'I do not know what you can wish for beyond what I am doing, and it seems to me that propriety does not permit of my doing more . . .'

" 'I touch neither your inclinations nor your heart,' he rejoined, 'and my presence causes you neither pleasure nor emotion.'

" 'You cannot possibly doubt,' she responded, 'that I am glad to see you, and I blush so often when I see you that you cannot doubt either that the sight of you causes me emotion.'

" 'I am not deceived by your blushes,' he answered. 'They come from a feeling of modesty, and not from your heart, and I infer from them only the part I really have in them.' "

As happens so often, Monsieur de Clèves' doubt keeps his love alive even beyond conjugal habituation.

"While he was her husband, he was none the less her lover, because he was always left with something to wish for beyond the mere possession of her, and although she lived on perfect terms with him, he was not entirely happy. He continued to feel for her a violent and troubled passion that cast its shadow across his joy."

If the husband and the wife are beings whose feelings go beyond average humanity, the lover, Monsieur de Nemours, has no less delicacy. The moment he falls in love with Madame de Clèves he conceals it from everyone and Madame de Clèves herself "would have found it difficult to perceive, if the inclination she had for him had not caused her closely to observe his actions, which left no doubt in her mind."

One other person has understood immediately what is happening: she is the one who always understands these things and who sometimes is heart-broken and sometimes rejoices, sometimes assumes the role of a duenna and sometimes that of a go-between; she is Madame de Clèves' mother. Madame de Chartres, on her death-bed, decides to speak to her daughter:

" 'You have an inclination for Monsieur de Nemours; I do not ask you to confess it; I am no longer in a state to make use of your sincerity to guide you. I have long been aware of this inclination, but I did not speak to you about it for fear of making you aware of it yourself. You know it only too well now; you are on the edge of the abyss; it will require great effort and drastic measures to save yourself. Think what you owe to your husband; think what you owe to yourself, and consider that you are going to lose that reputation which you have acquired and which I have so earnestly desired for you. Have strength and courage, daughter; withdraw from the court; force your husband to take you away; do not be afraid of taking too harsh and too difficult measures: however dreadful they may appear at first, they will be more pleasant in the end than the evils of an illicit love affair

31

. . . If this misfortune must happen to you, I greet death with joy, that I may not be here to see it.' "

It is seen how extreme the emotions are. Are there many modern mothers who would wish to die rather than to see their daughter dishonored? Notice also that pride plays a great role in these councils, and religion none, which is surprising. Madame de Clèves is warned to have care of her repute, not of her salvation. The romantics, two centuries later, were to "glory" in abandoning themselves to their passions.

Meanwhile Monsieur de Nemours succeeds in making Madame de Clèves understand that he loves her, and this without having said a word that could shock her, quite the contrary:

" 'Women,' he said, 'generally judge the love one has for them by the care one takes to please them and to seek their company, but this is not difficult if they be in the least attractive. What is difficult is not to give way to the pleasure of following them, to avoid them for fear of letting people see, and almost of letting *them* see the feelings one has for them. And what stamps still more an attachment as real is to become just the contrary of what one was, to have no longer ambition or pleasure, after having been busy all one's life with both . . .' "

Madame de Clèves understands only too well the share she has in these words.

"It seemed to her that she ought to reply and not tolerate them. It seemed to her that she ought not to understand them, or show that she took them as applying to her . . . The most obscure speech of a man one loves causes more agitation than open declarations from a man one does not love."

However she betrays herself through little things: Monsieur de Nemours while riding horseback with the King is injured, and Madame de Clèves betrays her apprehension, a scene which recalls to the modern reader that of the races in *Anna Karenina,* and which enables Monsieur de Nemours, on observing Madame de Clèves' pallor, to realize that he is loved as much as he loves. All these interpretations of pallors and blushes are shaded with infinite delicacy and resemble the minute analyses that make up the work of Marcel Proust.

Angry with herself for having let the secret of her love escape her, Madame de Clèves says to her husband that she wishes to leave for the country, that she is unwell, that she needs fresh air. Monsieur de Clèves, who sees that she has never looked better, does not take her seriously.

" 'Do not force me,' said she, 'to confess something I have not strength to confess, although I have several times intended to do so. Only remember that it is not prudent

33

for a woman of my age to be exposed to the dangers of the court.'

" 'What do you suggest to my mind, madame?' cried Monsieur de Clèves. 'I would not dare say it for fear of offending you.'

" 'Then, sir!' she answered, falling at his feet, 'I am going to make a confession such as was never made to a husband; but the innocence of my actions and of my intentions gives me the necessary strength. It is true that I have reasons for keeping away from court, and that I wish to avoid the perils that sometimes beset women of my age. I have never given the least sign of weakness, and I should not fear that I might do so, if you allowed me to withdraw from court . . . However dangerous may be the course I am taking, I am taking it gladly to keep myself worthy of you. I beg you to forgive me, if I have feelings that grieve you; at least I shall never grieve you by my actions. Remember that to do what I am doing requires more affection and more esteem for a husband than any wife has ever had: guide me, pity me and love me still, if you can . . .' "

Monsieur de Clèves is beside himself:

" 'I have never been able to awaken love in you,' he said, 'and I see that you fear you love another. And who, madame, is this happy man who gives rise to this fear? . . . I have at once the jealousy of a husband and of a lover; but it is impossible to entertain that of a husband after what you have just done.' "

She has barely spoken when she regrets it. She sees that Monsieur de Clèves is in despair, unhappy, that he imagines the evil to be more serious than it is, that he interprets a thousand little events of the past in the light of this passion, that he exaggerates them and is heart-broken.

"When the Prince had left and Madame de Clèves remained alone, when she considered what she had just done, she was so horrified that she could scarcely believe it was true. She felt she had destroyed her husband's love and esteem, and that she had dug for herself a pit from which she would never escape. She asked herself why she had done such a dangerous thing, and she discovered that she had committed herself to it almost in spite of herself. The strangeness of such a confession, for which she knew no precedent, convinced her of its danger."

Because she refuses to see Monsieur de Nemours, Monsieur de Clèves understands that he is the man in question:

" 'Would you dare refuse to see him if you did not know full well that he distinguishes your severity from incivility? But why need you be severe with him? From a person like yourself, madame, everything is a favor, ex-

cept indifference . . . I am the unhappiest of all men.
You are my wife, I love you like a mistress, and you love
another! This other is the most attractive man at court,
and he sees you every day; he knows that you love him.' "

Finally Monsieur de Clèves allows his wife to retire
to Coulommiers. There she receives a woman friend.
The latter, when she returns to Paris, innocently tells
that Madame de Clèves enjoys spending a part of the
night alone in the summer house in the forest of her park.
Monsieur de Nemours, who knows the place well, suddenly has the idea that it would not be impossible to get
a glimpse of Madame de Clèves there without being seen
by her. Monsieur de Clèves, who is present at this conversation, thinks he sees what is passing in Monsieur de
Nemours' mind, and has no doubt that the latter intends
to go and see Madame de Clèves. He is not mistaken, for
such is the effect of the design that has crossed Monsieur
de Nemours' mind. Monsieur de Clèves, in order to inform himself concerning his wife's conduct, sends one of
his gentlemen-in-waiting on Monsieur de Nemours'
traces.

Now Monsieur de Nemours goes to Coulommiers,
enters the garden, and stealing up to a small room he sees
Madame de Clèves there, "so beautiful that he could
scarcely restrain his rapture at the sight. It was warm, and
she had nothing on her head and shoulders but her loosely

THE PRINCESS OF CLEVES

bound hair. She was on a couch, with a table before her, on which were several baskets of ribbons." She chooses some, and Monsieur de Nemours sees that they are of the same colors as those he had worn at a recent tournament. For a long time she looks at a portrait, and Monsieur de Nemours observes that it is his own.

"It would be impossible to express what Monsieur de Nemours felt at this moment. To see in the middle of the night, in the loveliest spot in the world, a person he adored; to see her without her knowing that he saw her; and to see her wholly absorbed in things related to him and to the love she concealed from him—this has never been enjoyed or imagined by any other lover."

Madame de Clèves knows nothing of Monsieur de Nemours' presence in her garden that night. But Monsieur de Clèves, upon the report of it that is made to him, believes they have seen each other and cannot resist the overwhelming shock which this gives him. He is taken with fever that very night. Madame de Clèves is notified, and she arrives with all speed. And while she weeps, he says to her,

" 'You shed many tears, madame, for a death which you are causing, and which cannot give rise to the grief you show . . . Why did you reveal to me your love for Monsieur de Nemours, if your virtue was not strong enough to resist it? I loved you enough so that I would gladly have been deceived, I admit it to my shame; I have yearned for the false security which you destroyed. Why did you not leave me in that peaceful blindness which so many husbands enjoy? I should perhaps have been unaware all my life that you loved Monsieur de Nemours. I am dying,' he added, 'but know that you are making death welcome to me, and that after being deprived of the esteem and tenderness I felt for you, life would be hateful to me . . . Adieu, madame! You will some day miss the man who loved you with a true and lawful passion.' "

After this death, Madame de Clèves' grief exceeds the bounds of reason. Her dying husband—dying because of her and with so much tenderness for her—is always on her mind. She accuses herself, as of a crime, of not having felt love for him, as if that were a thing within her power. Monsieur de Nemours spends his life roaming about the walls that shelter Madame de Clèves. He thinks that since he is loved, she will marry him, now that there is no duty to oppose her feelings, and that the obstacles are removed. At last he can throw himself at her feet. She confesses to him that she loves him, that she has always loved him:

" 'I am willing that you should know it. I am happy to tell you. I am not even sure I am not telling you more from love of myself than from love of you. For, after all, this avowal will have no consequences, and I shall observe the strict rules my duty imposes.' "

Monsieur de Nemours rightly answers that she no longer has any duties.

" 'What phantom of duty do you oppose to my happiness? . . .' "

But she will not marry him:

" 'I know that he came to his death by you, and because of me . . .' "

In vain Monsieur de Nemours pleads the cause of passion. Madame de Clèves' sense of duty (or what she calls duty) triumphs:

" 'I admit,' she answers, 'that passions may lead me, but they cannot blind me. Nothing can prevent my knowing that you were born with all the dispositions for gallantry, and all the qualities likely to bring success therein. You have already had several love-affairs; you would have others, and I should no longer make you happy; I should see you become to another woman what you have been to me; I should be mortally hurt; and I should not even be sure of not suffering from jealousy.'

"Monsieur de Nemours was not yet put off, and he did all he could think of that might make her change her mind. At last, when whole years had passed, time and absence allayed his grief and extinguished his passion. Madame de Clèves so lived that there was little likelihood of her ever returning. She spent part of the year in the convent, and the rest at home, but in an isolation and in occupations more saintly than those of the most austere convents; and her life, which was brief, left examples of inimitable virtue."

5

This is the book which made such a great sensation when it appeared, which is considered today one of the masterpieces of the novel, and which a young man of our time, Raymond Radiguet, dreamed of imitating in *The Count's Ball*.

What did it contain that was new? First the simplicity of construction, which is worthy of the great tragedians of the same century. At one stroke, Madame de La Fayette defined one of the forms of the French novel. The natural, sober tone, the importance attached to feelings, the delicate and restrained analyses, the graceful brevity of the story, such are still the features of *Dominique*, of *The Double Misunderstanding*, of *The Pastoral Symphony* and of *The Death of Hippolytus*.

Madame de La Fayette was also the first to paint what may be called a society of leisure, and to describe the extreme delicacy of sentiments that can develop among men and women of noble soul when they have no other concerns but love. We have known societies of this type in France, and in particular in Paris, during the pre-war period; it will be very interesting, when we come to speak of Marcel Proust, to compare his description of the passions of the idle with that of Madame de La Fayette.

In Monsieur de Nemours and in Monsieur de Clèves, she has painted a somewhat conventional type of man, a slave of the manners he has imposed on himself, and in a language more abstract and pure than vigorous. A type that by its scruples might perhaps make more cynical generations smile, but that has its greatness. One can conceive more complete, more violent ones; one may prefer saints, sages or rebels. But it must be recognized that a society composed of such men represented quite a triumph of humanity over the human animal.

Was the triumph, perhaps, not too complete? Was the animal not too much sacrificed? And does not he who would play the angel play the fool? It surely cannot be said that the moral precepts which the heroes of *The Princess of Clèves* obey bring them much happiness. Monsieur de Clèves dies of grief, Madame de Clèves refuses the man she loves after having caused the death of the man she esteems and ends her life in remorse; Monsieur de Nemours is frustrated and never possesses the woman he loves. The failure could not be more complete. Must one conclude that so much nobility of soul was a fault? If Madame de Clèves had said nothing, and even if she had succumbed, would she not have done less harm?

Anatole France, in a preface which he wrote for an edition of *The Princess of Clèves,* relates that he asked a woman whose bold and penetrating mind he admired if Madame de Clèves had not put too high a price on virtue in thinking she was not paying for it too dearly with the death of a husband and the despair of a lover.

" 'The Princess of Clèves,' was the reply, 'is guided by wholly human considerations, without a trace of an ideal; wisdom and reason, which are temporal virtues, direct her life and rule her feelings. And even more than wisdom, it is the notion of her worldly greatness that penetrates and safeguards her. She worships appearances to the highest degree, and her beautiful attitude of haughty pride perhaps softens for her many secret griefs. I can imagine that to this lovely woman, whose psychology and especially whose morality were less complex than ours, the world must have appeared as a well-lighted drawing room which must be crossed with dignity and nobility. Then, with a majestic bow, one would retire and all was said. It is the triumph of etiquette, of an etiquette that can reach the point of heroism, for it sometimes takes more courage and firmness of soul to smile in the midst of a feast than on a field of battle. The Princess of Clèves has this kind of courage; she has it to the point of forget-fulness, to the point of self-immolation; she is without weakness, but also she is without pity. She lets two men despair and die, one at least of whom is loved by her. She is without remorse, since she remains irreproachable and nothing has seriously disturbed the fine ensemble of her conduct. She is a demonstration of what firm social con-victions and a severe rule of life can produce, without anything superior to those principles themselves. She is also an example, edifying perhaps but heart-breaking, of what morality and virtue can do for men's happiness. Before this honorable and pitiless soul one finds oneself considering those others, the heroines of love who were weak, who were guilty, but who were gentle. And one wonders if the root of this virtue was not pride, which consoled her for everything, and even for the harm she was doing? . . . ' "

This judgment has been criticized, and it has been maintained that Madame de Clèves' decision, inspired by a religious stoicism, is unintelligible to us only because we do not share her faith. But this is neglecting at once the text of the novel and the reactions of her contempo-raries. The conflict of the Princess of Clèves is that of passion and duty, but not of *religious* duty, for neither Madame de Chartres nor Madame de Clèves pose the question on this plane. What we have here is rather a

43

conflict of passion and of heroic pride, of what one desires and what one owes to oneself. The Church calls this form of self-love *human respect*.

It would be easy, in studying this conflict, to be rather hard on Madame de Clèves. The resistance, it might be said, is inversely proportional to the strength of the temptations. Racine's heroines succumb because they love passionately. Madame de Clèves resists because she knows nothing of sensuality. Her creator, Madame de La Fayette, as we have said, was nicknamed *le Brouillard*. What would have happened if she had been the *Tempest?* The heroine whom she has conceived dominates her instincts and her nerves every moment, but is not his "trembling" man's most human attribute? In Montaigne's words, *"Le tremblement n'est-il pas le meilleur de l'homme?"* La Rochefoucauld would no doubt have found more than one maxim on this subject.

"One always has enough strength," he might have said, "to overcome passions one does not feel." "More women are kept chaste by vapors and fever than by virtue." "One way of escaping from great emotions is to make petty crimes of them."

There are in truth two possible explanations of Madame de Clèves' conduct. Either her passions are weak or she possesses enough strength of character to overcome violent passions. We have been so long nourished,

THE PRINCESS OF CLEVES

through the Romantics, on the doctrine of giving free
rein to the passions that this hypothesis is the last one
we think of, but it is a very likely one. Torn between
desire and obligation, Madame de Clèves, a stoic and a
Christian, chooses obligation. One can find examples of
the same sublime purity in the work of Maurice Baring,
an English and Catholic novelist. And if one can deny
the wisdom of the posthumous obligation in which Madame de Clèves shuts herself up, one cannot deny its
grandeur.

But the novel raises another problem, and one of the
gravest moral and sentimental problems: that of total
sincerity. For Madame de Clèves could both remain
without reproach and be silent. It is her fatal confession
that causes so much mischief. The moment the book was
published (as we learn from M. Robert Lejeune, who has
written a remarkable preface to *The Princess of Clèves*)
this scene provoked endless discussions. People were so
divided that "they could have eaten one another." The
Mercure started a questionnaire. Madame de Gramont
answered that in such a case "a woman must examine
her husband's humor and temperament, for all husbands
are not alike." The men were rather of the opinion that
one should confess; women, that one keep silent.

If I did not fear to see the ghost of Madame de La
Fayette write "Rubbish" in the margin, I should be will-

ing to say that the danger of sincerity is that it is rarely sincere. I mean that before venturing to describe, for those who love us, feelings that can make them suffer so much, we should first be sure, (1) That we really experience them, and not merely imagine we do, or do so intermittently; (2) That the evil is without remedy; (3) That the character of our friends is such that they can bear sincerity. If these three conditions are fulfilled, then we may deliver ourselves of secrets which, in love as in friendship, are always difficult and heavy to bear. If they are not, let us have the courage to be silent.

Such are the reflections that the drama of *The Princess of Clèves* provokes in a moralist. But let us not forget that a fine novel is not a moral treatise. It describes a special case and does not propose rules for us. Madame de La Fayette and her characters offer the image of a world in which beings who had greatness tried to conduct their lives nobly, submitting their passions to honor and to duty. Being men and women, they were far from always succeeding, but being fallible ourselves, we must forgive them and be grateful to that French seventeenth century for having presented us one of the finest images of man in one of the finest of languages. Among the novels we shall study later we may encounter forms of love closer to those we observe today; we shall find none that have more grace, or modesty, and we shall not cease to think with respect and sympathy of those somewhat feverish evenings in a Paris of long ago where, near the gardens of the Luxembourg, in the time of Alceste and of Monime, two souls that were at once savage and tender engendered a heroic world.

TWO

ROMANTIC LOVE

Julia or the New Héloïse

ETWEEN THE *Princess of Clèves* and *The New Héloïse* it would no doubt be appropriate to devote a study to *Manon Lescaut*. The Abbé Prévost's book is one of the finest love-novels written in French and it affected the readers of the time as vividly as it still moves us. By the simplicity of its approach, the grace of its style, the naive strength of the passions it portrays, it already foreshadows Stendhal. But for our present purpose it seems that *The New Héloïse,* in spite of its defects, or perhaps because of them, is more representative of the eighteenth century. *Manon Lescaut* is a cry from the

49

heart, one of those masterpieces that are born of a great suffering and that are rather the reflection of an individual sensibility than of an epoch. For at least half a century *The New Héloïse* transformed the ways of love, the style and the vocabulary of the French. One cannot overlook it. But before speaking of *Julia* it will be well to trace the curve followed by the sentiments of love during the first half of the eighteenth century.

1. THE PERIOD

In studying *The Princess of Clèves,* we saw what happened to the passions of love in the seventeenth century, as they combined with the sentiment of honor. But this generation of "tamed lions" was bound to disappear rather quickly. We have described those half-pay soldiers of the heart of whom La Rochefoucauld is such a fine example. In the time of Louis XV the French public is composed of a court nobility and of a critical bourgeoisie who are both inclined to ridicule too stilted sentiments.

What becomes then of the passions of love? Heroic love, as we have observed in *The Princess of Clèves,* is replaced by love regarded solely as pleasure.

Gone are the tender respect that Monsieur de Nemours pays to Madame de Clèves, the proud chastity of

Madame de Clèves. Everything becomes free and bold. There is no more secrecy. Each one is proud to relate his adventures to all and sundry. Love, as Chamfort puts it, ceases to be anything but "the exchange of two fancies and the contact of two epiderms." Girls still read *L'Astrée,* or perhaps *The Princess of Clèves,* but they put them aside at the age of twenty. As soon as they are married the example and advice of those who surround them cause them to lose interest in romantic loves.

As the Goncourt brothers express it in their authoritative study, *Woman in the XVIIIth Century,* women forget "the tremulous avowals, the noble aloofness, the raptures awakened by innocent favors," the refinements of delicacy of a Madame de Clèves. "They lose all the illusions of the romantic, those tender reveries and the daytime languors, the sleepless and feverish nights, the torments of a first love." Like their whole period they yield to facile loves, and say to those for whom they may have had a fancy what Madame d'Esparbès said to Lauzun:

"Believe me, my young cousin, it is no longer the thing to be romantic. It makes you ridiculous and that is all. I had a fancy for you, my child. It is not my fault if you took it for a great passion, and if you got it into your head that it would last forever. It matters little to you, since this fancy has passed, whether I have taken another lover or remain without one. You have many advantages for winning women's favors. Make use of them to win them and be assured that the loss of one can always be repaired by another."

Thus women in the eighteenth century tend to adopt in matters of love the morals and the ideals of men. But this licentiousness produces effects which surprise the people of the time and which seem to us rather natural: namely, disgust with life and an invincible boredom. This is easy to understand. Nothing fills existence like a great love accompanied by doubts as to the feelings of the love-object. Everything then assumes an infinite value. Monsieur de Nemours (like Stendhal much later) could, I imagine, spend entire days meditating over a smile, a blush of Madame de Clèves, analyzing it, untangling reasons for hope and reasons for fear.

But what is more monotonous than licentiousness? What is more melancholy than the ceremonial of conquest, for those who have played that game all their lives? Add to this the fact that the times are irreligious. Human lives no longer have a fixed center to which the soul can cling. "Boredom is then a universal commodity of society." Books of piety and novels having disappeared from women's tables, they try to find reasons for living in scientific works. Great writers (Voltaire, Fontenelle) try to bring the new discoveries within their reach. They attend courses in Natural History. "A woman," says Goncourt, "no longer has herself painted on an Olympian cloud, but seated in a laboratory." The trouble is that in this laboratory she somewhat misses Olympus—and Jupiter.

Now each time men have experienced such a feeling of weariness they have tried to escape in time or in space. Of all escapes, the simplest seems to be the return to Nature. One becomes convinced that what surrounds one is boring because it is adulterated, but that men formerly have known happiness and that it would only be necessary to return to a simpler mode of living in order to regain a kind of balance. During the whole eighteenth century the French-style gardens of the seventeenth century give way little by little to English gardens, whose naturalness is indeed artificial, but creates an illusion. The time is not far distant when Marie-Antoinette, queen of France, will try in the hamlet of Trianon to convince herself she is a peasant woman.

What is true of gardens is also true of feelings. People try to recapture the freshness of their first passions. This explains the success of *Manon Lescaut*. "People came running as to a fire, because it *was* fire." The subject of *Manon Lescaut* is slight enough: the passionate love of a young man for a little courtesan. But the story is moving because it is naive and true. The libertine or the coquette who read *Manon Lescaut* must often have laid the book down on their lap and dreamt of the life of the Chevalier des Grieux, so unhappy and yet so happy, because a single emotion was enough to occupy him.

After escape to Nature, escape into Space, or exoticism. Every period afflicted with boredom gives itself over to this form of romanticism. This explains the vogue in the eighteenth century of the English novel, Chinese art, tales of travel, and the important place Savages hold in so many French books of the time. The Huron, "the gentle savage," is a fixed idea. It plays a role in the transformation of Rousseau's doctrine.

Thus, in a period of universal license, it is an escape to enjoy pictures of rustic scenes that have remained uncontaminated; in a period when passionate feelings are rare, it is a pleasure to study "emotional" beings (the word itself is to become fashionable); in a period of debauchery, it is a novelty to praise virtue. A mixture of virtue, of sentiment and of rusticity—this is a complex form of evasion, skilfully concocted, unconsciously apt; it is this mixture which brought the men and women of 1760 to Jean-Jacques Rousseau who, as we shall see, seems to have been created to bring them what they so badly lacked.

2. *THE MAN*

At the time Rousseau wrote *The New Héloïse* he was forty-five years old. Let us recall very briefly his early life. He was the son of a Geneva watchmaker and of a pastor's daughter. He had lost his mother while he was still a child; his father had had to flee as a result of difficulties with the authorities of Geneva. He himself, after having tried his hand at various callings, after having been a clerk, then an apprentice, had run away in turn and had begun his adolescence as a vagabond.

Born a protestant, he was taken in by some catholics living not far from the canton of Geneva who were dedicated to the conversion of children. He spent, at first, several weeks in the Seminary, where he became converted without great conviction, then was confided to Madame de Warens, who had him call her "Mother," took charge of his education and found him very gifted, a born musician. Madame de Warens was a maternal and sensual woman, whose heart was excellent but whose mind was somewhat wayward. She became Jean-Jacques' mistress though she did not love him, somewhat as George Sand became Chopin's mistress, with the feeling of accomplishing a duty, or rather using this supposed feeling to conceal her desire from herself.

On leaving her he pursues a thousand extraordinary occupations; he is secretary of a Greek archimandrite who is something of an ambassador, something of a thief, "engraver and lackey, musician and itinerant tradesman; and with it all, a dreamer, an artist, infinitely responsive to natural beauty and to simple pleasures, always looking with delight at the sky, the greenness or the water, rapt in the ecstatic contemplation of a secret dream". . . . When he arrives in Paris, in 1741, he has already led the life of a sentimental Gil Blas, of a moralizing Panurge. In a different time this background would have made a realistic novelist; in the eighteenth century it produces the first of the romantics.

Why has he come to Paris? He would have been hard put to it to say. He will suffer here, since he will be deprived of his trees, of his birds and his rivers. But he has read Plutarch deeply: he aspires to the glory of heroes . . . Glory? . . . What weapons does he dispose of to conquer it? He has invented a system of musical notation; he has written an opera, and although he has published nothing, he knows he is able to write. All this seems rather fragile.

As for the man, he is kindly, candid, capable of tenderness, but proud, touchy and suspicious. He lives in imagination more than in action: "One enjoys, not what one obtains but what one hopes for, and one is happy only before being happy." Such a man would be more at home in solitude, but there is his love of glory . . . Now it happens that this wished-for and improbable glory comes to him with surprising ease. Thanks to a few letters of introduction he obtains entry into the home of Madame Dupin, whose salon is frequented by all Paris, forms a friendship with her son-in-law, François, who is Madame d'Epinay's lover. Thus he is introduced to the "philosophic coterie." In 1750, the Academy of Dijon having announced a contest offering a prize for a discourse on the Sciences and the Arts, he writes his famous plea against civilization. To Greece, to Rome, to the eighteenth century, he opposes the simple humanity of the earliest times and natural virtue:

"O Virtue! are thy principles not engraved in every heart, and to learn thy laws does it not suffice to look into oneself and listen to the voice of one's conscience, in the silence of the passions?"

Did Rousseau believe these things at the moment he wrote them? However this may be, his eventual attitude was determined by that which he had taken in this debate. For his readers he has become the Man of Nature, the adversary of artificial feelings. This is his first claim to glory. In 1752 his *Village Soothsayer* is performed before the King with great success. The author is there, wearing the handsome beard of a savage. He appears an astonishing character; all Versailles is anxious to know him.

But this world that suddenly welcomes him so easily surprises him and is hardly of a character to please him. In his novel he has depicted the feelings of a simple man who, fresh from a rustic society, is introduced to the salons of Paris. Because he is well received he believes the friendships which he forms can grow without constraint; but women like Madame d'Epinay monopolize a friend every time they are bored, "which is always," and the literary coteries exact mutual admiration. Jean-Jacques soon wearies of the salons and he says so.

"Their discourse is neither made up of dissertations nor epigrams; they reason without argumentation and are witty without punning: they artfully unite reason and vivacity, maxims and rhapsodies; and mix the most pointed satire and refined flattery with strictness of morals. They talk about everything, because everyone has something to say; they examine nothing to the bottom for fear of being tedious, but propose matters in a cursory manner, and pass them over with rapidity: everyone gives his opinion, and supports it in few words; no one attacks with virulence that of another, nor obstinately defends his own . . . But, after all, what kind of knowledge do you think is to be gained from such agreeable conversation? To form a right judgment of life and manners; to make a right use of society; to know, at least, the people with whom we converse; there is nothing of all this: all that is here to be learnt, is to plead artfully the cause of falsehood; to confound, by philosophy, all the principles of virtue; to throw a false color, with the help of sophistry, on the passions and prejudices of mankind . . ."

These society people are machines that do not think for themselves, but are set going by springs:

"You need only inform yourself of their company, their clubs, their friends, the women they visit, the authors they are acquainted with; and you may immediately tell what will be their opinion of the next book that is published, the next play that is acted, the works of this or that writer they know nothing of, or this or that system of which they have not one idea. As ordinary clocks, also, are wound up to go but four-and-twenty hours, so are these people under the necessity of going every evening into company, to know what they are to think the next day. Hence it is, that there is but a small number of both sexes who think for all the rest, and for whom all the rest talk and act."

These observations remain essentially true. Social conversation is still hurried, brilliant and frivolous. Today as in Rousseau's time, whenever six Parisians get together they cannot converse for an hour without making hasty, witty and unfair judgments of half of Paris, "as though their hearts had nothing to communicate." The difference is that the life of our time is so difficult, so complex that our anguish saves us from boredom. In the time of Rousseau society people, and especially women, suffered from their frivolity, found a bitter pleasure in hearing themselves castigated and were only too willing to make a great man of anyone who would tell them harsh truths. Rousseau appeared at just the right moment. He would be the fashionable Savage. Unfortunately fashion changes quickly and society people were to weary of him as quickly as they had taken to him. But if the man Rousseau was to suffer from this, the work of Rousseau on the other hand was to conquer an empire more vast than the court and the city, and transform the ways of feeling for a whole century.

3.   L'ERMITAGE

In 1756, Madame d'Epinay offered to have fixed over for him a gardener's cottage that she owned in Montmorency. The property was called *l'Ermitage*. As he loathed the city, here was an occasion for him to become a real hermit. He accepted, but he did not go alone. There was a woman in his life: Thérèse Le Vasseur. He had met her in an inn where she was a sewing-maid. He had been struck by her modest demeanor, by her warmth and gentleness. A bond was quickly established:

"I declared to her in advance that I would not abandon her, nor would I ever marry her. Love, esteem, naive sincerity were the ministers of her triumph and it was because her heart was tender and true that I was successful without being forward. I had only sought to obtain a little amusement; I saw that I had done better than this and that I had provided myself with a companion . . . I wished to cultivate her mind. My efforts were wasted. Her mind is what nature has made it. Cultivation and training make no impression upon it."

Thus he found in Thérèse a companion for the body and for the heart, but not for the mind. One can imagine him during those first days in Montmorency, drunk with the country air, meditating in the loveliest season of the year, in the month of June, in the cool green groves, with the song of the nightingales, the babbling of the brooks:

"Everything conspired to plunge me back into the too seductive indolence for which I was born, but from which the hard times recently brought upon me by a long effervescence should have delivered me forever."

And so, free to roam in these lovely surroundings, he began to dream, and his reveries quite naturally found the path to love. What had he known of love? Small

adventures and great feelings. He still remembered with
emotion two charming young Swiss girls with whom one
day, in his childhood, he had taken the most innocent
walk . . . Naturally, Madame de Warens, the woman
who sinned through virtue . . . No doubt also a
Madame de Larnage, who had overcome Jean-Jacques'
timidity by taking the offensive herself . . . And this
was almost his whole love-past. He was timid, naive, but
exacting. Dressmakers, chamber maids, little shop-
women, scarcely tempted him.

"I had to have young ladies. It is by no means the
vanity of social class or rank that attracts me. It is a better preserved complexion, lovelier hands, a more gracious
manner of speech, a finer and better made dress, a more
dainty shoe, ribbons, lace, better groomed hair . . . I
always prefer the less pretty one having more of all this.
I myself find this preference quite ridiculous, but my
heart commands me in spite of myself."

His mind scoffs at society women; his desires go out
only to them. Now who are the women he knows intimately? Madame d'Epinay? He thinks he does not attract her. Besides, she is Grimm's mistress. And then he
does not actually want a real mistress. "One is only happy
before one is happy." In his dreams at *l'Ermitage* he imagines all the creatures who have aroused emotion in him

in his youth gathered around him, and he finds himself thus surrounded by a harem of former acquaintances.

"My blood kindles and sparkles, my head spins in spite of my graying hair, and behold the austere Jean-Jacques, at the age of nearly forty-five, suddenly become the extravagant shepherd again."

This intoxication is not sufficient to inspire him with the desire really to fall in love again:

"I felt too keenly the ridicule that an old gallant invites upon himself. I was not the kind of man who becomes more comely in his decline, having been little enough favored in my younger years. Besides, being fond of tranquillity, I should have feared domestic storms, and I loved my Thérèse too sincerely to expose her to the humiliation of seeing me feel livelier passions for others than those with which she inspired me."

What he wishes is a revery and, as often happens to artists, this revery soon assumes a constant form, that is to say, it becomes a work of art:

"I conceived love, friendship, those two idols of my heart, in their most ravishing images. I found myself adorning them with all the charms of the sex I had always adored. I imagined two friends, women rather than men, because this is more rarely to be found. I endowed them with two characters that were analogous but different, with two faces, not perfect but to my taste. I made

63

the one a brunette, the other a blonde, the one animated and the other composed. Taken with my two charming models, I identified myself with the lover and the friend as much as it was possible for me to do. I made him comely and young, giving him moreover the virtues and the defects that I felt in myself."

Finally, he seeks a setting for this dream. For some time he thinks of the Borromean Islands which he knows slightly, then of the valleys of Thessaly which he has never seen; he ends by choosing Lake Geneva, on whose shores he was born, and he sets up his two imaginary beauties in Vevey. For his own pleasure he makes his characters hold dialogues and he writes some of their letters—scattered letters, but which he was later to use. At the point he has reached he has to draw up a plot and find a title for his novel.

4. "LA NOUVELLE HELOÏSE"

The title is *The New Héloïse*. Why? Because the story he is going to try to write is, like the adventure of Héloïse and Abélard, that of a tutor who falls in love with the young girl entrusted to him. Thus Saint-Preux, a less timid Rousseau, is a tutor at Monsieur d'Etanges', a Swiss nobleman. He falls in love with Julia, the latter's daughter, and confesses his love in a letter. The novel opens with Saint-Preux's declaration to Julia. Saint-Preux, like Rousseau, is a sentimentalist; he asks for nothing. He simply wants to tell Julia that "her charms have dazzled his eyes."

"And why may I not suppose the same concord in our hearts, which in our judgment is so strikingly apparent? Sometimes it happens that our eyes meet; involuntary sighs betray our feelings, tears steal from . . . O! my Julia! if this unison of souls should be a divine impulse —if heaven should have destined us! . . . Shall I tell you, without evasion? When we are engaged in the puerile amusements of these long evenings, you cruelly permit me, in the presence of the whole family, to increase a flame that is but already too violent . . . Even yesterday you almost suffered me, as a forfeit, to take a kiss . . . I perceived by my increasing palpitation, that I was rushing upon my ruin, and therefore stopped in time. Ah! if at least I had dared to indulge my inclination, that kiss would have been accompanied with my last sigh, and I should have died the happiest of mortals . . ."

Barely has he written his letter when he regrets it:

"A hundred times a day I am tempted to throw myself at your feet, bathe them with my tears . . . But a sudden terror damps my resolution; my trembling knees want power to bend; my words expire upon my lips . . ."

Does she wish him to leave? He will go. This suggestion draws forth Julia's first letter:

"Be not too positive in your opinion that your absence is become necessary. A virtuous heart would overcome its folly, or be silent, and thus might become, perhaps, too formidable . . . But you—and yet you may stay."

Answer:

"I was a long time silent: your cold indifference forced me to speak at last . . . I must be gone."

Julia's second letter:

"No, Sir . . . A man, such as you feign yourself, will not fly; he will do more." (Which is an invitation to suicide.)

"Tomorrow you will be satisfied; and notwithstanding what you may then say, I shall have done less than it would be to fly from you." (That is to say, "I shall kill myself, and this is much less painful than to fly from you.")

Whereupon there is a third letter from Julia:

"Foolish youth! if my life be dear to thee, attempt not thy own!" immediately followed by a fourth: "Must I then, at last, confess the fatal, the ill-disguised secret! How often have I sworn that it should never burst from my heart but with my life! Thy danger wrests it from me. It is gone, and my honour is lost forever . . ."

Honor . . . For though they are passionately in love,

both want above all to remain virtuous. Julia wishes Saint-Preux not to leave her, but demands that he respect her.

"Thou shalt be virtuous, or be despised; I will be respected, or be myself again."

"Celestial powers!" cries Saint-Preux. "I possessed a soul capable of affliction, O inspire me with one that can bear felicity! . . . Your person will always appear to me, not only the most beautiful, but the most sacred deposit with which mortal was ever intrusted. My passion, like its object, is unalterably pure. The horrid idea of incest does not shock me more than the thought of polluting your heavenly charms with a sacrilegious touch: you are not more inviolably safe with your own parent than with your lover."

For the novel to develop, these heroes must have confidants. Whence a cousin of Julia's, Clara, and a friend of Saint-Preux's, who bears the strange name of Mylord Edward. For being virtuous one is no less a man and Julia, even though she wants to be respected, subjects her unhappy lover to very curious temptations. She makes a rendezvous with him in a grove, where, with Clara, she waits for him. This is the famous scene of Julia's Kiss.

"Soon as we entered, I was surprised to see your cousin approach me, and with an affected air of humility, ask me for a kiss. Without comprehending the mystery, I complied with her request; and, charming as she is, I never could have had a more convincing proof of the insipidity of those sensations which proceed not from the heart. But what became of me a moment after when I felt—my hand trembles—a gentle tremor—thy rosy lips—my Julia's lips touch, pressed to mine, and myself within her arms! Quicker than lightning a sudden fire darted through my soul. The fire issued with our sighs from our burning lips, and my heart sunk down oppressed with insupportable delight. When all at once, I perceived your colour change, your eyes close; you leant upon your cousin, and fainted away. Then fear extinguished all my joy, and my happiness vanished like a shadow. I scarce know anything that has passed since that fatal moment. The impression it has made on my heart will never be effaced. A favor?—it is an extreme torment— No, keep thy kisses, I cannot bear them—they are too bitter, too penetrating; they pierce, they burn to the marrow . . . They would drive me to madness."

These "bitter kisses" of Julia's aroused the mocking verve of Voltaire who, belonging to another generation, still regards love merely as a game.

In order to regain his calm, Saint-Preux has to travel. During his absence, Julia's father gives her to understand that he will never allow her to marry a man who is not of good birth. But on Saint-Preux's return, Julia becomes his mistress and immediately is overwhelmed with remorse:

"Inhuman as he is, let him fly from me forever, and deny himself the savage pleasure of being an eye-witness to my sorrows. But why do I rave thus? He is not to be blamed, I alone am guilty. I alone am the author of my own misfortunes, and can blame only myself for what has happened . . ."

Mylord Edward tries to convert Monsieur d'Etanges to the marriage, but in vain. Saint-Preux must leave Switzerland; he goes to Paris. Alas! Madame d'Etanges discovers the letters which he continues to write to Julia.

"All is lost! All is discovered! I no longer find your letters in the spot where I had hidden them. They were there still last evening. They can have been removed only today. My mother alone can have discovered them. If my father sees them, my life is done for! . . ."

Such are the two first parts of *The New Héloïse*. Rousseau carried these letters in his portfolio; he would read them to Thérèse and to her mother, Madame Le Vasseur, and they both wept over them. The author considered his novel finished and his two lovers forever separated, when a real episode occurred that gave the imaginary story a new span. And this is one of the examples in which one can perceive most clearly the curious collaboration of life and the novel, of imagination and reality.

5. *MADAME D'HOUDETOT*

Madame d'Epinay had a sister-in-law, Madame d'Houdetot, who like so many women in the eighteenth century did not love her husband, but was the mistress of Saint-Lambert, the officer-poet, Madame du Châtelet's lover.

"Madame d'Houdetot," Rousseau tells us in the *Confessions*, "was nearing thirty and was not beautiful. Her face was marked with smallpox; her complexion lacked delicacy; she was near-sighted and had slightly bulging eyes, but a youthful look for all that, and her manner, at once animated and gentle, was caressing. She had a forest of long black hair, naturally wavy, that reached down to her knees. She had a natural and very agreeable turn of mind; she played the harpsichord; she danced well, wrote rather pretty verses. As for her character, it was angelic; its essence was the gentleness of her soul. Except prudence and strength, it combined all the virtues."

This is a charming portrait. Now circumstances will that Rousseau's romantic fancy should attach itself to this woman. One day she drops in on him, during a rainstorm, all wet and muddy. Thérèse lends her some clothes. Another time she arrives on horseback, dressed as a man.

"Although I do not much care for such disguise," says Rousseau, "something romantic about this one caught me, and this time it was love."

Why did she keep coming back? Was it in order to inflame Rousseau? Not at all, though she must have taken a certain pleasure in seducing a man who was her sister-in-law d'Epinay's debtor and, in a sense, her property. The fact is that she came on the advice of Saint-Lambert, who knew Rousseau and had asked his mistress to go and see *le Solitaire* from time to time. She knew that Rousseau knew of her liaison with Saint-Lambert; she could speak to him without any embarrassment about her loves. It was natural that she should enjoy his company. But *le Sentimental* had not reckoned with his emotions:

"I was drunk with a love that had no object; this intoxication fascinated my eyes. I saw my Julia in Madame d'Houdetot, and soon I saw only Madame d'Houdetot, but endowed with all the perfections with which I had endowed the idol of my novel. To complete my undoing, when she spoke of Saint-Lambert it was as a passionate lover. Such is the contagious force of love that in listening to her I was seized with a delightful tremor that I had never felt in the presence of anyone. In short, without my noticing it, and without her noticing it, she inspired in me for herself all that she expressed for her lover."

Although deeply in love with Madame d'Houdetot, Rousseau is firmly resolved not to deceive his friend Saint-Lambert, and considers himself ridiculous besides for being afraid of succeeding in this.

"Am I then for Madame d'Houdetot a gallant much to be feared? Would one not think, by my presumptuous remorse, that my attentions might seduce her? Ah, poor Jean-Jacques! love to your heart's content and in the security of your conscience, and have no fear that your sighs will do Saint-Lambert injustice."

So, without fear, without remorse, he gives himself over to Madame d'Houdetot's friendship. She, like himself, is fond of taking walks; they take very long ones, in a land of enchantment. The women of the eighteenth century gladly granted small favors to the humblest aspirant.

"One evening, after having had supper alone together, we went walking in the garden in the beautiful moonlight. At the end of this garden was a fair-sized copse where we sought out a pretty grove—oh, undying memory of innocence and delight! It was in this grove while sitting with her on a grassy bank under an acacia laden with blooms that I discovered a language to express the impulses of my heart really worthy of them. It was the first and only time in my life, but I became sublime, if one can qualify thus all that the tenderest and most ardent love can convey that is most lovable and seductive to a man's heart. What intoxicating tears I shed upon her knees! And the tears I made her shed in spite of herself! At last, in an involuntary rapture, she cried,

" 'No! Never was a man so lovable, and never did a man love as you do! But your friend Saint-Lambert is listening to you, and my heart would not love twice . . .'

"I sighed and fell silent. I kissed her. What embraces! For six months she had lived alone, that is to say far from her lover, and from her husband. For three months I had seen her almost every day, and always with Love as a third party between her and me. We had supped together; we were alone in a grove, in the moonlight, and after two hours of the most animated and tender tête-à-tête she came away in the dark of night from that grove, and from the arms of her friend, as intact, as pure in body and in heart as she had entered it! Oh, reader, weigh all these circumstances. I shall add nothing more."

All this (which already anticipates Stendhal) very much resembled a situation in *The New Héloïse*, and undoubtedly Rousseau's regard for Saint-Lambert, and the virtue of all the actors in this strange comedy, remained unimpeachable. But such is not the opinion of the spectators. Madame d'Epinay, jealous of her sister-in-law, seemed annoyed and even furious. Thérèse Le Vasseur and Saint-Lambert both received revealing letters. The two of them vented their anger on Rousseau, who accused Madame d'Epinay of indiscretion and had violent quarrels with her. After this he could not continue to live at *l'Ermitage*. To him this was but new proof of the perfidy of all society.

Deprived of Madame d'Houdetot, whom he no longer sees since he no longer lives near her, and to whom he continues to write burning letters, he conceives the dream of living with her and Saint-Lambert, and the latter does not seem hostile to this extravagant plan.

"Her (Madame d'Houdetot's) feelings toward you have not changed," Saint-Lambert writes to Rousseau. "She loves you, honors you; it was I who brought you together and this is certainly not a matter for which I reproach myself. There is a constant desire in my heart to unite and bring together what I love and esteem most. I have always had a charming picture of spending my life between her and you, if we could induce you to live with her."

This, on the plane of the novel, is the source of the idea of marrying off Julia to a man as estimable as Saint-Lambert, and of bringing Saint-Preux into the household. In point of fact, the situations in reality and in the

74

novel are different, for Rousseau is to Madame d'Houdetot a quite harmless friend, while Saint-Preux has been Julia's lover. But Saint-Preux releases Julia of the vow she had made never to become the wife of another, and to obey her father she consents to marry Monsieur de Wolmar, a cold and reasonable man who is older than she, while Saint-Preux makes a trip around the world. When he comes back, after six years, he is received at the Wolmars' and Rousseau takes relish in describing the happiness of a virtuous family leading a simple and natural life far from great cities. This is the best part of *The New Héloïse*.

Julia's first conversation with Saint-Preux is attended with difficulties. At the moment when she tries to justify herself and to explain her marriage, Monsieur de Wolmar enters the room.

"What confounded me was, that she proceeded in the same manner as if he had not been there. He could not forbear smiling, on discovering my astonishment. After she concluded, he said: 'You see an instance of the sincerity which reigns in this house. If you mean to be virtuous, learn to copy it: it is the only request I have to make, and the only lesson I would teach you. The first step towards vice, is to make a mystery of actions innocent in themselves, and whoever is fond of disguise, will sooner or later have reason to conceal himself. One moral precept may supply the place of all the rest, which is this: neither to say or do anything, which you would not have all the world see and hear.' "

Everything that Saint-Preux discovers fills him with greater admiration for Wolmar's and Julia's wisdom. There is a famous letter on servants and the way to treat them, a fine description also of the garden that Julia has had made for herself and that she calls *L'Elysée*. But the calmness of their hearts is only apparent, and when Julia and Saint-Preux go for a boat-ride together it is not without melancholy that they think of the past.

"The equal and measured sound of the oars threw me into a reverie. The lively chirping of the snipes, recalling to my mind the pleasures of a past period, saddened me. By degrees I found the melancholy which oppressed me increase. A serene sky, the mild reflection of the moon, the silver froth of the water which sparkled around us, the concurrence of agreeable sensations, even the presence of the beloved object herself, could not banish a thousand bitter reflections from my mind."

In us, who have read Chateaubriand's *Memoirs from Beyond the Grave*, Victor Hugo's *The Sadness of Olympio* and Lamartine's *The Lake*, this note awakens familiar resonances; to the eighteenth century readers it appeared as a prodigy of sincerity, of passion and of freshness.

The novel ends with a fifth and a sixth part. Julia dies, advising Saint-Preux to marry Clara. She refuses. Saint-Preux and Clara will live on the memory of Julia, and bring up the dead woman's children. Although these concluding parts are less successful, the fact remains that *The New Héloïse* was the most moving, the most "novel," novel of the time. The manner might appear high-flown, but the emotions were true; the proof of this is that they affected a whole people.

6

How do the passions of love, as they are described in *The New Héloïse,* differ from heroic love as we have studied it in *The Princess of Clèves?* Sensibility has become more intimate. It is no longer the privilege of heroes. It is put within reach of all.

For Rousseau's characters are not heroes. Their natures are more susceptible than those of Madame de La Fayette's characters. The form itself is proof of this. However tense the situations in which they are involved, Madame de Clèves and her husband preserve a firm language, and if they die of grief they still maintain their dignity. Saint-Preux and Julia blend sighs and tears with their utterances. When they are moved, their sentences

77

are broken by sobs, exclamations and invocations. It is as if language, instead of imposing its rules on their thoughts, is molded to the impulses of their souls.

It is true that in the two novels the characters, instead of abandoning themselves to their desires, as those of so many modern novels would do, try to struggle. But in the case of Madame de Clèves the check is honor; in Julia's it is "virtue." It would seem that the first is much stronger than the second. Madame de Clèves remains irreproachable. Julia, at the first attack, not only succumbs but encourages her lover. If one compares the scene in the park of Coulommiers with that in the grove of Vevey the contrast is striking. Madame de Clèves does not know that she is seen by the one who loves her, and everything transpires in the realm of revery. Julia herself invites her lover and offers him the kiss which he dares not ask for. I do not speak of the men. Saint-Preux is a weak, or as Stendhal says, a rather contemptible fellow, while Clèves and Nemours are heroes.

But if we do not find, in these men and these women, the modesty of the great classics, neither do we find the naturalness of *Manon*, where passionate love did not awaken remorse, where the characters abandoned themselves to their desires without experiencing any moral sense. In Rousseau the idea of virtue is always present. What is this virtue? It is "the innate sense of doing

78

right." It is the natural or the divine law (for Rousseau these are one and the same thing).

He believes that man, if he can freely question his conscience, will without effort find the divine law. Why does he not follow it? Because society turns him away from it. It is only when Julia and Wolmar have chosen to live in the country that they can live according to nature —hence according to Virtue.

But is it true that men, freed from social temptations, are naturally virtuous? Are Rousseau's characters, a Wolmar, a Julia, quite human? I think Rousseau would have answered that they are much more human than the hypocrite or the libertine whom other authors of fiction depicted at the time. "Never," he says, "will La Rochefoucauld's melancholy book be enjoyed by good people."

And, on re-reading *The New Héloïse,* he has this to say:

"Having finished re-reading this collection, I believe I can see why its interest, however feeble, is so agreeable to me, as it will be, I am convinced, to every well-disposed reader: it is because this feeble interest is pure and unmixed with pain, because it is not aroused by means of villainies or crimes, nor mingled with the torment of hatred. I am at a loss to conceive what pleasure is to be found in imagining and composing the character of a scoundrel, in putting oneself in his place while one represents him, in setting him off in the most imposing light. I feel very sorry for the authors of so many tragedies full of horrors . . . As for myself, I am quite ready to admire their fine talents and their genius, but I thank God that he has not given these to me."

He is right. Good people exist. They scarcely appear in novels, because of the fear that they may bore readers, and because we all have a justified horror of hypocrisy. But good people are not necessarily boring. Monseigneur Myriel, in *Les Misérables*, Eugénie and Madame Grandet do not bore us. Far from it. False virtue is boring, not real virtue, which engenders serenity and joy. Virtue, to be lovable, needed only to have talent on its side. Rousseau put his heart into it and gave it victory.

7

The book's success was prodigious. It appeared at the opening of the Carnival:

"A pedlar brought it to Madame la Princesse de Talmont on a day when there was to be a ball at the Opera. After supper she had herself dressed to attend it. While waiting till it was time to leave, she began to read the novel. At midnight they came to announce that her horses were ready . . . She continued to read. Then her servants, seeing that she was forgetful, came to notify her that it was two o'clock.

" 'There's no hurry,' she said and continued to read.

"Some time later, her watch having stopped, she rang to find out what time it was. She was told that it was four o'clock.

" 'It's too late,' she said, 'to go to the ball. Have my horses put away . . .'

"She had herself undressed and spent the rest of the night reading."

All the women, and many young men, read *The New Héloïse* with the same fervor. The critics were more severe. Voltaire made fun of the style and tried to pass Rousseau off as a pretentious ignoramus, but the sentences that he makes fun of do not offend us.

On the subject itself Voltaire is equally sarcastic.

"The principal character," he says, "is a kind of Swiss valet who has studied a little and who teaches what he knows to Julia, the daughter of a Baron of the country of Vaud . . . The young valet spouts the morality of Epictetus to Julia and talks to her of love. Julia gives her teacher a long and very *bitter* kiss about which he does a good deal of complaining, and the next day the teacher gets his pupil with child. The ladies might suppose this to be the conclusion of the novel. But here, gentlemen, is the delicate plot, here is the wonderful philosophy that

81

enable this novel to go on for another five entire volumes after the conclusion . . ."

And Voltaire describes Wolmar saying to Saint-Preux:

" 'You have been my wife's lover; you will always be her good friend, but you will also want to be mine. We shall live together, all three of us, like good Swiss citizens, like good relatives, as though nothing had happened, and you can count on it that this little life will be a model of philosophy and of happiness.' "

Which is amusing, but unfair.

But if the critics were mocking and disdainful, the book's success was to be lasting. Almost all the men, not only of the eighteenth century, but of the beginning of the nineteenth, were molded by Rousseau. That master of tenderness and of sentimental revery taught Napoleon, perhaps Goethe, and even Stendhal how to love. Because he praised virtue he becomes a spiritual guide. Because he loved nature he teaches men the love of country life, the desire for a simple life. His sensibility, which was much more acute than that of a normal man, indeed almost pathological, becomes the rule and the model for several generations. In this sense it may be said that he was responsible for certain extremes of the Revolution, though rather by contagion than by influence.

And we ourselves, who scarcely read him and who miss a great deal in not so doing, what do we owe him? Has he transformed our way of love? He surely has. Jacques de Lacretelle—who, in a preface to the *Reveries of a Solitary Wanderer*—has written some of the most beautiful pages inspired by Jean-Jacques—rightly recalls that before him men did not dream of mingling nature with their feelings.

"Did trees and grass exist before Rousseau? One could almost say they did not . . . Sainte-Beuve calls attention to the fact that the first swallow in our literature is to be found in the *Confessions*. This is not quite exact: La Fontaine and Madame de Sévigné did see one or two." And I add, the poets of the *Pléiade*. But Sainte-Beuve is right in declaring that no one before Rousseau had written,

"Since I had been in Bossey, it was the first time I had seen greenness before my windows . . ."

"Now consider," says Lacretelle, "all the shades that have come from that greenness."

It seems to us today so natural to associate the memory of the birth of an emotion with that of a night walk in the woods, or that of the autumn of a passion with a walk in October in a park with yellowing leaves, that we forget that over a long period men had lost the habit of interweaving the poetry of things with that of the heart.

Proust may seem very far removed from Rousseau, but had it not been for him, would he have thought of making the description of the hedge of hawthorns coincide with the first appearance of Gilberte Swann?

The history of sentiments, like that of political events, is not simple. The currents mingle, vanish, and nothing would be more erroneous than to say, "After a period of licence and of frivolous love, the eighteenth century adopted the passionate lyricism, the combination of sensuous delight and of virtue which constituted love *à la Rousseau*." That there were libertines after Rousseau as before him is proved by Laclos' fine book, *Dangerous Relations*, which appeared in 1782.

THREE

LOVE AS WARFARE

Dangerous Relations

T̶HE NEW HÉLOÏSE is one of the aspects of love in the eighteenth century, *Dangerous Relations (Les Liaisons Dangereuses)* is another. Rousseau, a romantic, runs away from his time and pictures love as he would wish it; Laclos, a realist, observes his time and pictures love as he sees it. Truth to tell, he depicts it in a very restricted environment which is aristocratic society. It is a world in which men and women enjoy leisure, in which the necessity for earning a living is unknown, in which the game of politics that fills so large a place in the life of modern man is forbidden, in which the so-called "ruling" classes have nothing to rule. What shall one do,

85

when one has nothing to do, if not make love? Love then becomes a game, like chess, in which possession is equivalent to a check-mate. After which each one seeks a different partner and tries out the same gambits all over again. It is monotonous, melancholy, often cruel. "But what do you expect?" the author seems to say; "that is how men are."

1. THE AUTHOR

Who was this author? General Choderlos de Laclos. But he became a general only late in his career. At the time when he wrote his famous novel (1782) he was still a subaltern stationed in the provinces. In Grenoble, which was the best garrison in France for society and amusement, the local nobility had taken some notice of this tall and lean young man, with his pale complexion, his blue eyes, his fiery, sensitive soul. He was a passionate admirer of Rousseau and also of Richardson. He had read and reread *Clarissa Harlowe*; it was partly in order to create a French Lovelace that he wrote *Dangerous Relations*.

Was he himself a Don Juan? It seems not. One of his biographers tells us that just as Stendhal waged war in the Commissariat, so Laclos made love in the Information Bureau. He liked to talk to ladies and receive their confidences. Women confide more readily in those non-combatant observers than in the great love-conquerors. Henry James and Marcel Proust both had a mad craving for gossip. It is of small gossip, in fact, that great novels are sometimes made. An anecdote becomes the point of departure for a scene, for a chapter. Later on the people of Grenoble were to recognize, or think they recognized, some of the characters of *Dangerous Relations* and help to make the book a success.

The picture of French society which Laclos presents is very harsh. "One of the greatest defects of novels of this kind," says La Harpe, "is that they pass off the story of a handful of fops and whores as representative of the *mores* of the century." Nothing is truer, especially in France. Between the two wars, from 1920 to 1940, we saw in Paris a small group of thirty or forty people fill the whole scandalous chronicle with their amorous permutations. The rest of the nation led normal, affectionate family lives, but led them without fanfare, while the little group of cynics filled the gazettes with the reverberations of their adventures.

The novelist is more inclined to write about the prostitute than about the saint. The events in the life of the former are more numerous. Besides, in the eighteenth century a man like Laclos, in describing "high society," had a tendency to exaggerate its dark side. The Revolution was already smoldering beneath the ashes of the bourgeoisie. A poor officer like himself had bitter grudges against the great noblemen. *Dangerous Relations* is, in a sense, in novel form what *The Marriage of Figaro* is on the stage: a pamphlet against the depraved nobility. Not that a word of politics is to be found in it, but it is a documentary indictment in the file of the class that the Revolution will attack.

Like *The Marriage of Figaro,* the book created a furore among those very people against whom it was aimed. Everyone, in Paris and in Versailles, wanted to know the author. His Colonel became concerned. An officer who was a novelist and a libertine . . . This did not look too well. But Laclos was an excellent artilleryman, and the novel got by on the strength of his proficiency with cannon. Although the characters had been observed in Grenoble, people of taste recognized the book as the work of a moralist and the characters as timeless. Of this the author himself was conscious. "I have preferred," he tells us, "drapery that I could keep before my eyes; the experienced man easily strips the model and recognizes the nude." Valmont and Madame de Merteuil are types as much as, even more than, they are portraits.

The strange thing is that this successful author, after one triumph, wrote nothing else. Artillery won the day,

and love. For the creator of Valmont married and became the happiest, the fondest of husbands. We have his
letters to his wife, whose maiden name was Soulange-
Duperré, and who was the sister of the Admiral of France.
"For nearly twelve years it is to you that I owe my happiness," he writes her. "The past is the guarantee of the
future."—"I am glad to see that at last you feel you are
loved, but allow me to tell you that for the last twelve
years you can have had no occasion to doubt it." He
praises her for being "an adorable mistress, an excellent
wife and a tender mother." Is she getting fat? "The more
there is of you, the better it is." And this is not a case of
an aging lion, since this exclusive passion has lasted for
twenty years.

In his old age, after the Revolution, in the course of
which he had been an agent for the Duke of Orleans,
Laclos thought of writing another novel to prove "that
there is no happiness outside of the family." André Gide
rejoices that this project was not carried through, and
does not believe for a moment that Laclos, agent of
mysterious intrigues and cynical novelist, can sincerely
have loved virtue. "There is no doubt," says Gide, "that
Laclos was hand in glove with Satan." After having read
his letters, I am not quite so sure. But that he knew
Satan well and that he painted admirably the hell of
love-as-pleasure is proved by the reading of his only book.

2. THE BOOK

Dangerous Relations is a novel in the form of letters. This is a somewhat artificial form, for after all the essential part of life is not put into letters, but it is a convenient form, because it always allows speaking in the first person (which is technically easier) while entering the consciousness of diverse characters. Laclos congratulates himself on the variety of styles which he lends to his characters. This variety does not strike us so much and all of them—or almost all—are too clever. It is true that in the eighteenth century everyone, in this circle, was clever and the merest chit of a woman in those days would make more than one writer of our time turn pale with admiration and envy. Laclos writes extremely well, in that pure and abstract language that is so appropriate to the analysis of sentiment, which La Rochefoucauld, Madame de La Fayette, La Bruyère and Pascal had molded. Gide in this connection brings up the name of Racine and it is a fact that one thinks of Racine more than once in reading *Dangerous Relations*.

The chief characters are: The Vicomte de Valmont, a professional Don Juan, expert and diabolical; the Marquise de Merteuil, who is a feminine double of the same character and even more diabolical than Valmont; the

Présidente de Tourvel, a beautiful commoner, devout and prudish; Cécile de Volanges, a naive young girl, just freshly out of the convent, whom her mother would like to marry off as soon as possible to the Comte de Gercourt, but who loves the young Chevalier Danceny; this Chevalier finally, a mere child, who loves Cécile, but whom Madame de Merteuil, without loving him, has as a lover. Cécile's mother and a few confidants make up the minor characters.

The plot is intricate, for if the book has but one subject, which is the danger of certain relations, these relations themselves are numerous and curiously involved. To begin with, it happens that Gercourt, whom the young Cécile is to marry, has been Madame de Merteuil's lover and has betrayed her in a manner which she has never forgiven him. Madame de Merteuil, a pitiless woman, desires vengeance. In order to obtain it she turns to Valmont, who has also been her lover, but who has remained her friend and accomplice. Between Valmont and Madame de Merteuil there is no vain hypocrisy. Both of them are cynics; they have had pleasure together; perhaps they will have it again; all without love. They work together for certain operations, as bandits may do, without mutual confidence but with professional esteem for each other.

"You know," she writes to Valmont, "how much store

Gercourt sets by the purity of the woman he will marry. Seduce the Volanges girl before the marriage and let us make a fool of our enemy . . . Besides, the heroine deserves all your attentions; she is really pretty—just fifteen: a real rose-bud."

Valmont at first displays little zeal. Seduce a girl who has not seen anything, who does not know anything? Is this an enterprise worthy of a man like him?

"No," he answers Madame de Merteuil. "I am involved in an affair whose success will bring me both glory and pleasure . . . You know the Présidente Tourvel, her devoutness, her love for her husband, her austere principles. This is what I am attacking; this is an enemy worthy of me; this is the goal I plan to pursue."

At this moment he is in the country, in a chateau, with an aunt of the President's wife, where the latter is also staying, and the siege of the devout woman completely absorbs him.

Madame de Merteuil is indignant. A Valmont at the feet of the Présidente Tourvel, of that woman completely devoid of charm, laughably gotten up. On her side the Présidente receives letters in which she is warned against Valmont, but she defends him with a warmth which already betrays her interest:

"He speaks to me with great confidence, and I preach to him with great severity. You who know him will agree how splendid it would be to convert him. . . What I can assure you is that being constantly with me, seeming even to enjoy my company, he has not let escape a single word that resembles love. . . He is perhaps a little flattering, but with such delicacy that he would accustom modesty itself to praise."

When the Devil assumes the garb of a hermit he can teach lessons to saints.

The three plots interweave. Danceny, separated from Cécile, entrusts Valmont with delivering his letters to her. At this point the conquest of Cécile begins to interest Valmont. Betraying a friend lends spice to the seduction of an innocent girl. Using the pretext that he finds it difficult to deliver the letters to her in broad daylight, Valmont obtains from Cécile the key to her room. He comes there one night, very scantily clad, sits down on the girl's bed, steals a kiss, then much more, and he finds himself the lover of a charming girl, whose heart remains faithful to Danceny, whose body belongs to Valmont and who, with a natural unconsciousness, with a candid duplicity, accepts this strange sharing. Each night from then on she happily welcomes Valmont, who methodically depraves her, and each day she writes Danceny letters full of tenderness.

This success does not prevent Valmont from pursuing the conquest of the Présidente. He has reached the point of speaking to her of love, of making her listen. For a moment she recovers herself and tries to escape him by taking flight. Resistance then exasperates desire.

"Now I shall never be happy or content until I have possessed that woman whom I hate and love with equal fury. My fate will become endurable to me only the moment I can dispose of hers. Then, tranquil and content, I shall see her in turn delivered to the torments that I suffer at this moment. . . That time will come."

He has reason to hope, for the unhappy Présidente loves him with desperation. How to bring about the downfall of the unfortunate woman? Valmont's arsenal contains classic weapons. He pretends that out of despair he is resolved to withdraw from the world, perhaps to a monastery. Deeply touched, the timid woman receives him. "Possess you or die," he tells her. She still eludes him. In a low and sinister voice Valmont murmurs, "Then it is death!" She falls fainting into his arms. He has his victory.

Then comes the time of chastisement. The Présidente, believing herself to be adored, quickly discovers that Valmont, having won her love, remains the libertine he has always been and is making sport of her. He sends her a most cruel letter. Utterly beside herself she enters a convent: "Leave me, cruel one! Farewell, sir," and she dies there after having learned of the death of

Valmont, killed in a duel by the Chevalier Danceny who has discovered the whole truth from a package of letters. Cécile, dishonored, takes the veil. Madame de Merteuil, who is the author of so many evils, catches smallpox; she survives it, but is disfigured, having lost one eye and become hideous. What a fatality!

"And who could fail to shudder when he considers the misfortunes that a single dangerous relation may cause?" Thus ends this quite immoral morality. The scene is strewn with corpses and with nuns. One is reminded of the last act of *Hamlet*.

3.   THE CHARACTERS

Are these characters true to life? Yes—so much so that we have met them, not in life but in history. Valmont in certain respects is Byron; Madame de Merteuil, without her perfidiousness, is a mixture of Lady Melbourne and of Lady Oxford, one of whom was the confidant and the other one of the mistresses of Byron. Re-read the correspondence between Byron and Lady Melbourne. You will see that they speak about the games and campaigns of love in the same vein as Valmont and Madame de Merteuil. It is the same conscious, detached attitude of the technician who considers all resistance merely as a difficulty to be solved and which his experience will be able to overcome. There is, to be sure, the difference that Byron is less cynical than Valmont, that he spares Lady Frances Webster while Valmont corrupts Cécile, that he is ready to throw his heart into the game and that his victims have almost always picked it up and even run away with it. But Valmont himself is not very far at times from being in love with the Présidente. Madame de Merteuil alone knows nothing of pity, nor of love, and it is a fact that certain women are more adept than men at a ferocious realism, free of all sentimentality.

Byron had read Laclos and it is possible that the character of Valmont, like that of Lovelace, may have had some influence on his actions. Young men are apt to copy the heroes of novels. But what explains Valmont himself? Is it natural for a human being to be as consciously evil? In particular is it conceivable that a man should be so cruel in love, which in most others arouses tenderness? This is the whole problem of the Don Juan and it must be recognized that Don Juan is a classic, universal character, who has always powerfully attracted men and women. How is a Don Juan born? How is a Valmont formed? The case of Byron helps us to understand this. Byron, born sentimental, becomes a cynical seducer the day the first girl he has sincerely loved be-

96

trays him. In the war that he wages on women there is an element of revenge. He will no longer be their dupe because he has been it once.

Another element in the formation of Don Juan is the too passionate search for the ideal woman. Don Juan appears to despise women; it is often because he has expected too much of them. At the beginning of his life he goes from woman to woman in search of love. Subsequently the mechanical side of adventures gets the upper hand. Don Juan discovers the power and the sureness of his technique. He then desires to make use of it, in part because he finds pleasure therein, but especially because thus he satisfies his pride; he is like those conquerors who attack innocent countries because they have a good army and are proud of it. Valmont is a condottiere of love. He is even capable of placing his talents at the service of a foreign power. "Conquer Cécile," Madame de Merteuil tells him. And he will conquer Cécile, because his "glory" is involved.

His vocabulary is that of the warrior:

"Up to this point, my lovely friend, I believe you will find I have adhered to method with a consistency that will delight you; and you will see that I have in no way deviated from the true principles of this kind of warfare, which we have often observed to be so similar to the other. Judge me therefore as you would Turenne or

SEVEN   FACES   OF   LOVE

Frederick the Great. I have forced the enemy to give combat when he was trying to gain time; by skilful maneuvers I obtained for myself the choice of terrain and of dispositions; I was able to lull the enemy into a feeling of security, the better to pursue him in his withdrawal; I was then able to follow this up with terror, before engaging in combat; I have hazarded nothing, except in consideration of a great advantage in the eventuality of success, and the certainty of resources in case of defeat; finally I have opened action only after assuring myself of the possibility of retreat, enabling me to cover and keep all that I had previously won."

In love as in war, every ruse is permissible.

Thus the first stage in the evolution of Don Juan might be disappointment in love; the second, the triumph of technique. The third is boredom. Technique has its pleasures, but they are monotonous. The progressive phases of a conquest, ever identical, no longer suffice to distract Don Juan. He knows too well that a given gesture will yield him a kiss, and a given scene a mistress. He craves novelty, and it is thus that he comes to seek the spice of cruelty. To triumph over innocence, over religious scruples, helps to offset the insipidity of love-feasts. Valmont derives pleasure from Madame de Tourvel's torments:

"Yes, I like to see, to contemplate this prudent woman,

unwittingly committed to a path which allows of no return, whose steep and dangerous slope draws her in spite of herself and forces her to follow me. There, terrified by the peril she is running, she would like to stop and cannot hold herself back. Her caution and her skill may indeed make her steps shorter, but they must follow one after the other. Sometimes, not daring to look the danger in the face, she shuts her eyes and, letting herself go, commits herself to my care. More often a new fear revives her efforts: in her mortal fright she makes still another effort to turn back; she exhausts her strength climbing up a short distance; and soon a magic power brings her again closer to the danger that she had vainly tried to flee."

He enjoys teaching the young Cécile a kind of catechism of debauchery:

"Nothing is more amusing that the ingenuousness with which she already uses the little she knows of this language! She cannot imagine one's speaking in any other way. The child is really seductive! The contrast between naive candor and the language of depravity produces the most curious effect, and, I hardly know why, only bizarre things still delight me."

Finally, as a supreme refinement, he amuses himself when he is in bed with a harlot by using her posterior as a desk on which to write to the Présidente:

"Never have I had so much pleasure in writing to you; never, while engaged in this occupation, have I felt emotion at once so sweet and so vivid. Everything seems to augment my rapture: the air that I breathe is full of voluptuousness; the very table on which I am writing you, dedicated to this use for the first time, becomes for me the sacred altar of love; how greatly it will be embellished in my eyes! On it I will have traced the oath to love you always! Forgive, I beg you, the disorder of my senses. I should perhaps not let myself be so carried away by raptures which you do not share: I must leave you now a moment to dissipate an excitement which is growing every moment and which is becoming greater than I can bear."

But Valmont would be less evil if there were not Madame de Merteuil. He retains a certain sentimentality for which she disdainfully reproaches him:

"But what I have said, what I have thought, what I still think, is that you are none the less in love with your Présidente; not, indeed, a love that is either very pure or very tender, but of the kind of which you are capable; of the kind, for instance, that makes a man find in a woman charms and qualities she does not possess; that sets her apart and relegates all others to a second order; that keeps you still attached to her, even while you outrage her; such in short as I can imagine a Sultan may feel for his favorite Sultana, which does not prevent him from often preferring a simple odalisque."

Madame de Merteuil, on the other hand, is pure evil, without a trace of feeling, without a shadow of pity. She seeks pleasure, to be sure, but this is not her crime. Even more than pleasure, she seeks triumph, domination, and the moment she encounters resistance, she craves vengeance; she must have had in her childhood some dreadful inferiority complex that can find its compensation only in the most cruel revenges. To ruin men and women, to place some in ridiculous situations, and others in tragic situations, to drive them to dishonor and to death, herein lies her happiness.

She derives all the more enjoyment from her depravity as she has managed to create for herself, in the eyes of society, the character of a virtuous woman. While she receives lovers in her little house, the devout praise her strictness. She pushes hypocrisy to the point of genius and thereby judges herself much stronger than Valmont.

"And what have you done," she writes to him, "that I have not surpassed a thousand times? You have seduced, even ruined many women, but what difficulties have you had to overcome? . . . As to prudence, adroitness, I do not speak of myself, but what woman would not have shown more than you?"

One seems to hear the accents of Corneille:

And what have all those years done to merit such praise
That is not more than equalled by one of my days?

    Et qu'a fait après tout ce grand nombre d'années
    Que ne puisse égaler une de mes journées?

Once again, this is the vocabulary of the warrior. And Valmont and Madame de Merteuil in effect oppose each other like two excellent gladiators, like two fencers of genius. Perhaps some day they will meet again, as adversaries worthy of each other. The reader already knows that Madame de Merteuil will win. In this war of the sexes, the man who encounters a beautiful, brilliant woman, one who does not lose her head, is only a novice. He understands this so well that in all his novels, in his poems, he preaches sentiment and even passion to the woman, for he knows that the day the woman no longer seeks anything but pleasure—or pride—the man becomes her slave.

And yet this ferocious Amazon can, when she wants to, be a woman. When Madame de Merteuil puts herself out to please, she prefigures certain of Stendhal's women (Duchess Sanseverina, Lamiel):

"As we had six hours to spend together, and as I had resolved that all this time should be wholly blissful, I would moderate his raptures and change my mood from

tenderness to coquettish playfulness. I do not think I
ever took such pains to please, nor was ever so satisfied
with myself. After supper, by turns childish and reasonable, sprightly and loving, sometimes even licentious, I
enjoyed thinking of him as a Sultan in the midst of his
harem, of which I was by turns the different favorites.
And indeed his repeated homages, though always received by the same woman, were always received by a
different mistress."

As for Cécile, she is perhaps Laclos' masterpiece.
Barely out of the convent, she reveals herself after her
first experience to be devilishly sensual and wonderfully
cunning in her behavior. Madame de Merteuil had
judged her well at the first glance.

"She is truly delightful! The minx has neither character nor principles; you can imagine how pleasant and
easy she will be to get along with. I don't think she will
ever shine on the side of sentiment, but everything about
her promises the liveliest sensations. Lacking adroitness,
she nevertheless has a certain natural falseness, if I may
say so, which sometimes even astonishes me, and which
will succeed all the better since her face offers the image
of candor and ingenuousness. She is naturally very passionate, and I sometimes amuse myself with her: it is
incredible how easily the little thing gets aroused, and
then she is delightful, for she knows nothing, absolutely

nothing, of what she is so eager to know. She gets fits of impatience that are quite funny; she laughs, she frets, she weeps, and then she begs me to tell her things, with a really seductive openness. I tell you I am almost jealous of the man who has this pleasure in store for him."

There remains the Présidente de Tourvel, who is everything that Madame de Merteuil is not—tender, sincere, faithful, unhappy, and capable of dying of love. But the Présidente is a commoner, Madame de Merteuil a great lady, and herein is to be found, as we have said, the key to the book, which denounces the immorality of high society.

The French Revolution was directed against political abuses, but also against depraved morals. Puritanism has its faults; it does not beautify life; but it gives singular force to a ruling class. The licentiousness of the rulers engenders anger, contempt, and in the end the revolt of the ruled. Laclos admires his monsters, but he condemns them.

4. THE MORALIST

It is customary to regard *Dangerous Relations* as an immoral book. The truth is that it is a moralist's book. Now a true moralist always depicts an immoral world, because he puts us on our guard against the world as it is. If nature were moral, morality would not exist, nor would moralists. But nature is immoral, or amoral, and societies have imposed morals upon it. The great moralist always frightens, because he is true, and truth is frightening to man. When he expresses himself in abstract aphorisms, the moralist's hardness appears less crudely. It is nevertheless present. Imagine, as you read La Rochefoucauld, the novels he might have written. You will find a hundred *Dangerous Relations*.

Love as Laclos describes it, and as the eighteenth century practiced it, might be called love-as-warfare, or love-as-pleasure. It proceeds from the same intellectual processes as the ideas on politics of the men of the same period. The omnipotence of reason was the religion of that time and the human spirit confidently expected to regenerate society, sentiments and morals *a priori*.

Centuries of civilization had constructed "edifices of enchantment": kingdoms, families, moral codes. The eighteenth century (or at least the most characteristic of its masters) wishes to make a new departure and to listen only to reason.

What does reason in fact say to a Valmont or to a Merteuil?

a) Pleasure is a positive good that one must try to experience as often and as intensely as possible.

b) If a woman refuses the quest for pleasure, the

man's role is to convince her. To do this he must strike
down her defenses: religion, fear, sexual modesty, faith-
fulness. This is what Madame de Merteuil applies herself to in the case of the young Cécile:

"Well, my dear! So you are very angry, very much
ashamed! And that Monsieur de Valmont is a wicked
man, isn't he? What? He dares to treat you like the
woman he would most love! He teaches you what you
would be willing to die to find out! Such behavior is indeed unforgiveable! And you, for your part, want to keep
your learning for your lover (who does not take undue
advantage of it), you cherish only the torments of love,
not its pleasures! Nothing could be finer, and you will
figure admirably in a novel. Passion, misfortune, virtue
above all, how beautiful they are! In the midst of this
brilliant parade one is sometimes bored, to be sure, but
one repays it in kind."

c) The rules of vulgar morality are not applicable to
certain beings who soar above these platitudes. A Merteuil considers herself liberated from all the verbiage of
sentiments:

"Ah! keep your advice and your fears for those de-
lirious women whose exalted imagination would make
one believe nature has placed their feelings in their
heads; who, having never reflected, continually confuse
love and lover; who, in their mad illusion, think the one

man with whom they have sought pleasure is its sole dispenser; and who, like the true superstitious creatures that they are, reserve for the priest the respect and the faith which are due only to the Deity. . .

"But what have I in common with those thoughtless women? When have you seen me deviate from the rules I have prescribed for myself and fail in my principles? I say *my principles,* and I say it advisedly: for they are not, like those of other women, given by chance, received without examination, and followed out of habit; they are the fruit of my deep reflections; I have created them, and I may say that I am my own creation."

"I am my own creation . . ." These beings are created out of principles and reason. Applying logic to what instinct should dictate; feigning passions one does not feel, in order to assure oneself pleasures which one considers the only realities; coldly studying the weaknesses of others in order to dominate them, such is the game played by Merteuil and Valmont. Can it procure happiness? Laclos' novel shows clearly that it cannot. Not that there is not a delightful reality in pleasure. But Madame de Merteuil herself ends by recognizing that physical pleasures are monotonous if they are not animated by the strength of feelings:

"Have you not noticed that pleasure, which is indeed the sole motive of the union of the two sexes, does not yet suffice to form a relation between them? And that if it is preceded by desire, which draws them together, it is no less followed by disgust, which repels them from each other? It is a law of nature that love alone can change; for can love be summoned at will? Yet there must always be love, and it would really be very embarrassing, if it had not been discovered that fortunately it need only exist on one side. The difficulty is thereby diminished by half, and at that there has been little to lose; in fact, the one enjoys the happiness of loving, the other that of giving pleasure; a little less keen, to tell the truth, but added to which is the pleasure of deceiving, to balance it; and everything works out."

But alas, everything does not work out. The one who does not love yearns for an emotion he does not share; he who loves wearies of an emotion which is never shared. As for Merteuil and Valmont, if they have come together in the war of the senses, only hatred and rivalry can grow out of their association.

"Tell me, Vicomte, which of us two will take it upon himself to deceive the other? You know the story of the two knaves who recognized each other as they met at the card table. 'We won't do anything,' they said to each other. 'Let's share our stakes', and they left the game. Believe me, let us follow this prudent example, and let us not waste together a time we could employ so well elsewhere."

Technique no more takes the place of love than propaganda takes the place of faith.

5

This, then, is the balance-sheet of the eighteenth century in the history of sentiments. Love-as-pleasure, as set forth in *Dangerous Relations*, engenders a dismal and mechanical monotony; love-as-delirium as set forth in *The New Héloïse* neglects too much the realities of the flesh. Is it possible to unite them? Is it possible to be an intelligent technician of love, and at the same time a passionate lover? Is it possible to admire at once Saint-Preux and Valmont, and to blend them into a single character? The answer must be sought in the novels of Stendhal.

FOUR

PASSIONATE LOVE

The Heroines of Stendhal

E HAVE DISCUSSED so far forms of love that are linked to a time, to historic circumstances, to a state of society. *The Princess of Clèves* was the expression of a whole generation's taste for heroic love; *The New Héloïse*, of another generation's craving for sentiment; *Dangerous Relations* expressed a reaction of the bourgeoisie on the eve of the Revolution against a cynical conception of love which, together with other wrongs and injustices, was identified with a decadent nobility.

The conception of love which is expounded (both in didactic and in novel-form) in the work of Stendhal is also in part that of his time. But even more, it is that of a certain type of human being, a type that may exist at any period, that exists in ours, and of which Stendhal was one of the most remarkable exemplars. It is not that of Rousseau; it is not that of Laclos; it is neither pure sensibility nor pure cynicism, but it is a mixture of the two. It is the conception of a man who is tender, melancholy, naively adroit, too intelligent not to be a little cynical, too sensitive not to forget his cynicism when he wishes. It is therefore necessary, before studying the heroines of Stendhal and his ideas on love, to give a brief picture of the man.

1. THE AUTHOR

It will be remembered that his name was Henri Beyle, that he was born in Grenoble, in 1783, and that he was deeply marked by his family on both the mother's and the father's side. His father's family, the Beyles', represented everything that Stendhal was later to hate. His father, Chérubin Beyle, was a not too kindly man who thought about nothing but acquiring or selling domains, excessively wrinkled and ugly, stiff and silent with women, who were nevertheless necessary to him. Chérubin Beyle was very devout, and no less so was his sister, the Aunt Séraphie whom Stendhal for a long time considered his evil genius.

To make up for this he deeply loved his mother, who was pretty, who died young; his maternal grandfather, Gagnon, a man of the eighteenth century, with a powdered wig and a three-cornered hat, who professed a philosophy modeled after that of Fontenelle, and his Aunt Elizabeth Gagnon, who handed on to him what he later called his *espagnolisme*, that is to say a sense of honor like that of the Spanish nobility, of the kind that Corneille for example shows us in the *Cid*.

"She formed my heart. Her character was the quintessence of honor. She communicated this manner of feeling to me. This it was that caused me to commit a ridiculous series of stupidities, out of delicacy and magnanimity."

Through his father's family and the tutor whom they chose for him, Stendhal is a persecuted child—persecuted with hypocrisy, with the sweet words of solicitude. Right away he forms the idea that humanity is composed of two distinct groups: the *Knaves*, who endlessly talk about virtue, but are hypocritical and base, and the *Generous Souls*, who are romantic, loving, but cynical in speech through fear of hypocrisy. His hatred for the Knaves and his love for the Generous Souls quickly reach the extreme violence of childish passions.

This violence remains with him. Stendhal is capable of wishing death to those he detests. At the moment of the Revolution and the Terror, Henri Beyle becomes passionately republican because Chérubin Beyle is a monarchist. One day his father comes home to announce the execution of King Louis XVI: "They've done it!" he cries, "They've murdered him! . . ." Stendhal tells us, "I was swept by one of the most tumultuous bursts of joy that I have experienced in my life." This seems cruel, and it *is* cruel. But Stendhal was always to admire the violence of the Renaissance, and extreme characters who do not recoil before assassination, less out of wickedness than through horror of weakness and contempt for the sceptical indulgence that had characterized his grandfather Gagnon and that had allowed the latter "neither to sense error nor to combat it".

"Weak beings seem to me mad," writes Stendhal, who yet on several occasions proved himself weak in love. But his taste for the violences of the Renaissance and for energetic souls will find expression in the characters he creates. Julien Sorel and Fabrice will kill. The Duchesse Sanseverina will resort to poison. Mathilde de la Mole will kiss dead lips. Lamiel will love a thief and herself become an incendiary. In the work of Stendhal will be found not only *espagnolisme* but also the *mores* of the Italian chronicles of the fifteenth century. In it Macchiavelli and Borgia join hands with Corneille.

In Stendhal the man, however, this violence never assumes the form of action; which is one reason why it finds an outlet in the novel.

As concerns love, Stendhal also receives two different educations which both come to him from the Gagnon side. His aunt Elizabeth Gagnon, as we have seen, taught him love *à la* Corneille. His uncle Romain was, like his grand-father Gagnon, a man of the eighteenth century, something of a libertine, who taught him a kind of art of love not unlike Ovid's, or Valmont's.

"It is curious," says Abel Bonnard, "to consider that the two influences of the libertine uncle and the romantic old maid explain everything that love meant to Stendhal."

He brings to it, in fact, an astonishing combination of strategy and timidity. Why is he timid, since he is addicted to strong characters? He is timid *precisely* because he is a passionate character, because he attaches too much importance to women and to love, because he has too much imagination. When he meets a new woman, he expects so much happiness from her that the moment he approaches her and begins to know what she is really like, he trembles as though he were on the edge of a divine mystery. *Divine* is a word that he constantly uses, and never with reference to God. This quite naturally accounts for his timidity.

Stendhal wrote a parallel between the character of Werther and that of Don Juan, and he chose to oppose in this work two aspects of his own character. Should one treat women as Don Juan or as Werther does, should one act toward them like a conqueror or like a sighing lover? Stendhal is not without admiration for Don Juan, who has in his favor courage, vivacity, coolness, amusement, absence of hypocrisy.

"It is true that the Don Juans have a very melancholy old age, but most men do not reach old age . . ."

At bottom humanity respects Don Juan, even while blaming him, whereas the sighing lovers, the Werthers, lay themselves open to ridicule. But this is of little importance. They are happy; they build castles in Spain, in which happiness dwells. "Werther's kind of love opens the soul to all the arts, to all sweet and romantic impressions, to the enjoyment of the world in all its forms." Don Juan considers women as enemies. Love, in his eyes, is a war and he speaks only of "victories." But it is the Werthers who really taste the joys of love.

Besides, one does not choose one's own temperament. Jean-Jacques Rousseau and the Duc de Richelieu could not have exchanged roles in their relations with women. Stendhal does not blame the Duke for having been a

Don Juan. He does not attach great importance to love that is only physical desire, but he thinks that the Duke never had moments like those that Rousseau experienced, in a grove, with Madame d'Houdetot. And I am quite inclined to agree with him. Rousseau remembers all his life a dress lightly touched, a hand softly pressed, while Richelieu no longer even knows, when he meets a woman, whether she has once been his mistress. "To tremble is the better part of man."

What accounts for the fact that the Werthers are happier is that Don Juan "reduces love to the level of the ordinary. Like a general, he thinks only of the success of his maneuvers." The Werthers are happy through sympathy and tenderness. La Rochefoucauld himself has said,

"The pleasure of love is to love, and one is happier by the passion one feels than by that which one inspires."

Don Juan's happiness is only sensuality, a brief thrill, and above all vanity, while the happiness of the Duc de Nemours, when Madame de Clèves tells him she loves him, "is above the happiness of Napoleon at Marengo." Love à la Don Juan resembles the passion for hunting. It is a need of activity, that must be awakened by diverse objects. Love à la Werther is a new goal in life; it changes the face of everything. Everything becomes new, living, moving:

"A mistress aspired to for three years is really a *mistress* in the full force of the term. The Werthers approach her only with trembling. . . . The man who trembles is not bored."

The pleasures of love are always in proportion to fear. The danger of inconstancy is boredom, the monotony of the operations, the yawning that succeeds victories, as is well shown in *Dangerous Relations*; the danger of passion is despair and death, as we have seen in *The Princess of Clèves* and *The New Héloïse*.

Stendhal himself will waver all his life between Werther and Don Juan. Through temperament he rather inclines to Werther; but thanks to the lessons of his uncle Gagnon, and thanks also to the company of men like his friend, Mérimée, he *wants* to think as a cynic. He does not want to be a dupe. This is a duty he imposes on himself. He has difficulty in fulfilling it, for Stendhal is a tender soul, and he is lacking in vanity. Don Juan is proud. . . But Werther! . . . He is much too afraid of displeasing. Stendhal is indifferent to the pleasures of ambition and of pride. His real need is the need to admire: his dream, which he will never realize, is a mutual passion with a "divine" or "sublime" woman. He is in love with love.

Such is the nature, such are the aspirations of Stendhal. Let us now look at his doctrine.

2. *THE MECHANISM OF THE PASSIONS*

On the mechanism of the passions of love, Stendhal has very precise theories and to learn what they are we need only analyze his essay *On Love.*

"Love has always been for me," he writes, "the most important, almost the only thing."

He dedicated a whole book to it and his novels, his *Diary,* are but long commentaries on this passion. He distinguishes four forms of it: passionate love, which is the love of Monsieur de Nemours, of Saint-Preux, or of Héloïse for Abelard; love-as-inclination, much less intense, which is like a painting into which nothing disagreeable must enter; physical love, which is self-defining; and finally love-as-vanity. Of these four forms of love the only one which Stendhal considers to be true love is passionate love. How is passionate love born? He has described it in the famous chapter on "Crystallization". This, says Stendhal, is what takes place in the soul:

"1: Admiration. 2: You say to yourself, 'What a pleasure it would be to kiss and be kissed by her.' 3: Hope. 4: Love is born. 5: The first crystallization begins. You adorn the woman you love with a thousand perfections. After twenty-four hours of exposure to love, this is what happens in a lover's mind: If you throw a branch shorn of its leaves by winter into a deserted pit in the Salzburgh salt-mines, when you recover it two or three months later you will find it covered with brilliant crystallizations. The tiniest branches, those that are no bigger than the leg of a titmouse, are adorned with an infinity of quivering, fiery diamonds. The original branch is no longer recognizable. What I call 'crystallization' is the operation of the mind that draws from everything it is confronted with the discovery that the loved object has new perfections. If you are in love, and a traveler talks to you about Italy, you think,

" 'How happy I would be to go there with the woman I love.'

"A friend of yours breaks his arm at the chase; you think,

" 'How sweet it would be to be cared for by that woman!' "

Alain has remarked that crystallization is not a mechanical, but a voluntary process. One must be in love with love in order to crystallize. And yet if one remained at this stage of love, the soul would grow weary, for it wearies of everything that is uniform. But this is followed by:

"6: Doubt. After having conceived hope, the lover suddenly encounters indifference. He comes to doubt his happiness. He wants to fall back on the other pleasures of life. He finds them annihilated. 7: Then begins the second crystallization, which is a constant reflection on the loved object, the lover roaming ceaselessly between these three ideas: 'She has all the perfections. . . She loves me. . . But what must I do to obtain proof of this love from her? . . .' "

If the woman is so careless as to kill all fear by the explicitness of her avowals, the crystallization ceases for a moment. But love then acquires the charm of a limitless confidence. If it succeeds in triumphing over boredom, constancy in passion becomes possible.

If she should leave you, the crystallization begins again, and the thought of each joy she could give you concludes with this heart-rending reflection, "I shall never experience that joy again!"

Crystallization is more rapid in woman than in man, because the woman has more time to crystallize. A woman who is sewing, or who has her embroidery frame before her—an insipid work occupying only her hands—thinks of the man she loves while the latter, galloping across the plain with his squadron (today we would say, "driving his car"), is put under arrest if he makes a wrong move.

Stendhal still believes, unlike many modern writers, notably George Bernard Shaw, that in love the man attacks while the woman defends herself; that the man asks and the woman refuses; that the man is bold and the woman timid. In Bernard Shaw, the woman thinks, "How shall I get him to commit himself?", and the man, "How can I keep my freedom?" In Stendhal the man says to himself, "Shall I be able to win her favor?", and the woman thinks, "Isn't it just a game he is playing when he says he loves me? . . . Can I trust him?" Women are more timorous because opinion means more to them. "They cannot, like men, quell opinion by risking their lives. They must therefore be much more on their guard." In them the intellectual processes that accompany the birth of love are more delicate, more timid, more slow.

The arts, and particularly music, help to promote crystallization by bringing back the memory of the loved one. The same kind of pleasure is to be found in the novel. To read a love story is to steep oneself again in the loves we ourselves have known, and especially in the one we are living at the moment.

"I have just this evening discovered that music, when it is perfect, puts the heart in exactly the same situation as when it enjoys the presence of the loved object, in other words that it gives what appears to be the most intense joy that exists on this earth."

Beings who are a prey to passionate love live in a state of consuming fever.

"If you know that tonight you will see the woman you love, the anticipation of so great a joy makes all the moments that separate you from her unendurable. And when you see her? You are embarrassed, silent. The moment the too lively interests of his passion are involved, a proud and sensitive soul cannot be eloquent in the presence of the loved one. Vulgar souls, on the contrary, calculate their chances of success; they possess assurance. The tender soul must resign himself to receiving nothing but charity from the loved one. His only resource is to try to be natural."

Everyone becomes more lovable for being natural.

"I don't love you," says Lamiel to the Duke. "You don't seem true and natural. You always seem to be acting a part."

The Stendhalian lover appears natural whenever he forgets his vanity to think only of his love. This type of love refuses to share its place with any other passion. He who experiences it is proud of sacrificing to it all the rest. He feels himself more noble, better by his disdain of all prudence and all pride. Happier, too, because man is always happier when he can give his actions a single goal, attach those actions to a fixed center. Doubt, which is always painful, is then overcome. Passionate love becomes, for a great character, a necessary and sufficient reason for living.

3. *REAL LOVES*

Did Stendhal himself encounter passionate love?

The first woman to excite him to feelings of love was a rather pretty actress of the theatre in Grenoble, Mademoiselle Kably. This was a schoolboy love. He was sixteen. He did not know her at all, but the violence of his feelings was so great that he did not even dare to watch for her in the street and that the one time when he met her by chance he nearly fainted. This passion was so lively that he even forgot for it his hatred of his Aunt Séraphie. But he would go to see Mademoiselle Kably at the theatre and applaud her, and would tremble when he heard her name. It was a curious adventure for this woman, to have become famous for stirring love in a child whose name she perhaps never heard. When Mademoiselle Kably left Grenoble, Stendhal consoles himself (in his silent manner) with the sister of a friend of his, Victorine Bigillion. Then he leaves for Paris and for Milan. In Milan he falls in love with a very beautiful woman, Angela Pietragrua, but he does not dare to declare himself.

Coming back to Paris, he meets another actress, Mademoiselle Louason, whose real name was Mélanie Guilbert. To pay court to Mélanie, who must not have been excessively shy, Stendhal resorts to a uselessly complicated strategy. But no matter, since he derives his pleasure precisely from the obstacles he invents! He speaks of Mélanie as one of his novel-heroes would speak of Madame de Rênal or of Clelia Conti. At this point the Diary is altogether delightful:

"I went to Mélanie's, a little trembling. I blew up the fire myself. This task, announcing intimacy, delighted me. We stayed together until two o'clock. I was very happy and I would only wish that she had been as much so as I . . . She was divine when she was telling her stories. I sat beside her, looking straight at her, not missing a single one of her features, holding her hands in mine. She certainly felt that her tender soul stirred me. The joy and excitement that she showed on seeing me seem to prove that she loves me. Yet I had bored her a little the last time, for as I said to her, 'Let's choose a sign that you will make me when I bore you,' she merely said, 'Ah, yes!' with a note of satisfaction. This sign is the question, 'Is there a ball at the Opera?' But at least I twice made her laugh heartily. I am beginning to get back my composure. I still have moments, however, when only my mouth is talking, while my heart is busy

feeling. Then it always keeps harping on the same
idea . . ."

And a few days later:

"I have just come from Louason's . . . I believe I have
never shone as I did tonight, nor played my role so well.
I wore a waistcoat, silk breeches and black stockings, with
a cinnamon bronze coat, a handsomely tied cravat, a superb hat. And never, I believe, has my ugliness been
more completely effaced by my animation. My whole
soul shone through, so that the body was forgotten. I appeared a very handsome man, in the style of Talma . . ."

I like that naive self-satisfaction of a timid, too-modest
lover. One is reminded of Rousseau writing, "That night
I was sublime . . ." after the scene in the grove with
Madame d'Houdetot. Unhappy mortals spend their
lives trying to find reassurance in themselves.

Stendhal conquered Mélanie Louason in the end, "in
spite of his strategy", and in 1805 he joins her in Mar-
seille. Back in Paris, he falls to a new passion: the wife
of his protector, Madame Daru. At last he returns to
Milan and there he again meets Angela Pietragrua, who
is now married and to whom he confesses that he formerly loved her. She scarcely remembers this fun-loving
young man whom she used to call le Chinois.

"Why didn't you tell me?" she asks with surprise.

But Beyle, consumed with tenderness, with modesty,

with respect for beings who expected neither respect nor modesty from him, was always to find it infinitely difficult to talk.

"This madness gave me a few moments of the most divine illusion, which the very ones who were the cause of it never suspected, or could not understand."

Angela (or rather an Angela born of his imagination) always remained in Stendhal's eyes the ideal mistress—dark, superb, voluptuous. He had loved her from 1800 to 1811, without ever seeing her, which had rendered the *crystallization* particularly easy. When the real Angela entered his life he discovered that she was deceiving him shamelessly, and broke with her. He then had, in Milan, a new love, for Mathilde Dembovska (whom he calls Métilde in his Diary), a platonic love but one around which, once more, he wove marvelous feelings.

In his life there are in all eleven women—whose initials, when he reaches the age of fifty, he draws in the sand with his cane. Few of them had loved him, and indeed he speaks of their feelings toward him with great modesty. Like all true lovers he is without vanity, even in his choices, for the mistresses of this man who was so tender were very commonplace, at least in beauty. But he wanted only to find beautiful souls. He believes he found them. In fact, he created them. Of Mélanie Guilbert he says, "Beautiful is not the word, but 'sublime'".

Of another, "I should not have believed that such a beautiful character existed in nature". In truth these women who fill Henry Beyle's life are already heroines of Stendhal.

Let us now see how he imagines love, when he is altogether free to create.

4. THE HEROINES

Stendhal creates the heroines of his novels above all to please himself. They are therefore "great souls", but belonging to two different classes. There will be, on the one hand, *the woman Stendhal would have liked to love,* tender, modest, passionate, concealing her passion, pious —because it is an additional triumph for the lover to overcome her piety; in short, perfect and yet vanquished by passion. Such are Madame de Rênal in *The Red and the Black,* Clelia Conti in *The Charterhouse of Parma,* and also a woman of whom we shall say little because her portrait is scarcely drawn and the novel in which she figures is merely sketched, but who belongs to the same breed, Madame de Chasteller, in *Lucien Leuwen.*

The second type is *the woman Stendhal would have been* (or Julien Sorel would have been) if he had been a woman, in other words, "a soul of the Renaissance".

Such are Mathilde in *The Red and the Black,* la Sanseverina in *The Charterhouse of Parma,* and Lamiel in
the novel that bears her name.

It is in *The Red and the Black* that the two types are
depicted with the greatest frankness. Let me recall the
subject as briefly as possible. In the time of the Restoration (1814-1830) Julien Sorel, the young son of a peasant, sensitive and courageous, full of enthusiasm for
Napoleon and of hatred for all those who may consider
themselves his masters, enters the home of Monsieur de
Rênal as a tutor. The latter is a squire in the province of
Dauphiné, married to a woman who in her extreme timidity is greatly disturbed at the thought that a stranger is
going to come between her and her children.

"Womanly delicacy was pushed to an extreme point
in Madame de Rênal. Her mind had formed the most
disagreeable picture of a crude and unkempt creature,
hired to scold her children solely because he knew Latin."

She is charmed when she discovers that Julien Sorel
is only a very young peasant, who looks almost like a girl
in disguise. He hates her because she is a rich man's
wife; he considers her contemptuous, because she is taci-
turn. In reality Madame de Rênal is "endowed with a
delicate and disdainful soul".

She does not love Monsieur de Rênal, who treats her

with haughty condescension and considers it quite natural that she should be devoted to him. She cannot imagine that other men may be different from her husband. She believes they are all crude, insensitive to everything that is not money-interest, or precedence, or decorations.

"The blind hatred of any reasoning that did not fall in with their ideas would have appeared to her as natural to their sex as the wearing of boots and a felt hat."

If she had been a Parisian woman and had read novels, she would have understood, on seeing Julien, the danger to which the young man's coming into the house might expose her, but "everything moves slowly in the provinces, where there is so little that is natural". Madame de Rênal has never experienced love, but she does not know it. Thanks to her ignorance, she is perfectly happy in Julien's presence, though immediately drawn by him.

She discovers this penchant in herself when her chambermaid indicates a desire to marry Julien. To her own surprise she becomes indignant. "Could it be that I feel love for Julien? . . ." She is both happy and anxious. The countryside appears to her in a fresh light. Her admiration becomes rapture. There can be no doubt. She is crystallizing. Julien, out of pride and not love, makes it a point of honor to win her affections. One evening in the garden, in the darkness, as he is in the midst of gesticulating, he touches Madame de Rênal's hand which is resting on a wooden chair. This hand is quickly pulled back. But Julien thinks it is his duty to bring it about that this hand be not withdrawn when he has touched it. The following evening he comes back with the look of a man who is going to fight an enemy. As soon as night falls, he takes the hand of Madame de Rênal, who withdraws it. Julien, without knowing what he is doing, again seizes it.

"A last effort was made to take it from him, but finally this hand remained in his."

Julien's soul is flooded with happiness—not that he loves Madame de Rênal, but because a horrible torture has just ended and he has a feeling of victory. He is still at the stage of love-as-vanity. Madame de Rênal on the contrary, with her hand in Julien's, thinks of nothing, just lets herself drift on life's current; already passionate love seems natural to her, and when an accidental circumstance obliges her to withdraw her hand, she gives it back subsequently without protest. Naturally Julien becomes emboldened.

" 'What?' Madame de Rênal said to herself, 'could it be that I love, could I feel love, I, a married woman, could I be in love? But I have never felt for my husband anything like this dark madness that makes me not want to let Julien out of my thoughts. After all, he is a child full of respect for me; this can be only a passing madness . . .' "

Hardly does she see him again when her whole soul is lifted by the magic joy that has astonished her for the last two weeks.

"As Madame de Rênal had never read any novels, all the shades of her happiness were new to her. No melancholy truth came to congeal it, not even the specter of the future. She imagined herself as happy in ten years as she was at this moment."

Julien plays the rôle of seducer out of duty: he forces himself to be bold.

"Madame, tonight at two o'clock I shall come into your room."

He trembles lest his demand be granted. When two o'clock strikes he again experiences that frightful sense of a duty to be accomplished toward his pride and he goes into Madame de Rênal's room. There is a little disorder.

"Julien forgot his vain plans, and resumed his natural rôle. Not to win such a charming woman's favor would have seemed to him the greatest misfortune."

A few hours later, when he leaves the room, he has nothing more to desire. Madame de Rênal is unbelievably happy.

"She could not get over her astonishment that such

happiness could exist and that she had never had any suspicion of it."

He himself at last falls desperately in love. He is young; she is charming; vanity yields.

" 'It must be admitted,' he would say to himself, 'that she is good and kind as an angel, and no one could be prettier . . .' "

Julien's love-as-vanity here tends toward passionate love. Madame de Rênal's tender rapture is all the more "sublime" in Stendhal's eyes as the remorse of this virtuous and pious woman is more vivid. One enjoys triumphing only over resistance.

"Her life became heaven and hell. Hell when she could not see Julien; heaven when she was at his feet."

" 'I no longer delude myself,' she would say to him, even in the moments when she dared to give way to her love . . . 'I am damned, irretrievably damned. You are young, you yielded to my seductions. Heaven can forgive you, but I am damned. I know it by a certain sign: I'm afraid. Who would not be afraid at the sight of Hell? But after all, I don't repent. I would commit my fault all over again, if I had it to commit.' "

Naturally the servants gossip. Monsieur de Rênal's enemies write him anonymous letters. Madame de Rênal shows an extraordinary presence of mind in defending her happiness and Julien's security. Byron had already noted the astonishing resourcefulness in intrigue, the bold courage, shown by the most virtuous women the moment they really experience a great love. Julien himself is frightened.

" 'I find you both illuminated and blinded by your love,' he said to her. 'The way you behaved today was admirable, but is it wise for us to try to see each other tonight? This house is lined with enemies . . .'

" 'So, you don't even have courage!' said Madame de Rênal with all the haughtiness of a woman of rank.

" 'Actions speak louder than words,' said Julien, 'let the world judge.' "

And he comes back. But this time Monsieur de Rênal takes steps to force Julien to leave the house. The reader will see Madame de Rênal again only at the end of the book. One must remember, in order to understand the last scene in the novel, so often criticized, that Julien passionately admires Madame de Rênal (as he admires Napoleon) *because she is a great soul.*

Arriving in Paris after a few years spent in a seminary, Julien becomes the secretary of the Marquis de la Mole, and here meets the second heroine of the novel, who is the Marquis' daughter, Mathilde de la Mole. Mathilde is an extremely beautiful, ravishingly blond girl. The first time Julien meets her he does not like her. He thinks

he has never seen such beautiful eyes, but he finds that
they betray great coldness. She has received a monarchic
and religious education, but she reads Voltaire. She possesses the qualities of her breed to a too high degree not
to be shocked by the weaknesses of her class. She despises the young men of rank who surround her, being
unfortunate enough to have more wit than they. At
least Julien Sorel is not like the rest. She makes advances to him. He thinks,

"How I dislike that tall girl!"

There is certainly some affectation in this noble aloofness. In vain Mathilde treats him to a eulogy of Rousseau. Julien's eyes remain penetrating and severe. She
is all the more surprised at this as it is usually she who
produces such an effect on others. She feels herself despised by Julien, and she cannot despise him. She cannot
endure this man's look of disapproval; she is afraid of it.

Looking at her, he thinks of Madame de Rênal.

"What haughty disdain! How different she is from
the one I have lost! How charmingly natural she was,
how unaffected! . . . I would relish her thoughts before she spoke them. I would see them come into being.
My only antagonists in her heart were her children,
which is a reasonable and natural affection, endearing
to me even though I suffered from it. I was a fool. The
ideas I had formed about Paris prevented me from ap-

preciating that sublime woman. Great God, what a difference! And what do I find here? Vanity, dry and haughty, all the shades of self-love, and nothing more . . ."

The colder and more respectful he is with Mathilde, the more she is after him. A double *crystallization* begins:

"God, how beautiful she is! . . . How much I like her big eyes, when I look at them closely, scrutinizing me as they so often do."

He wakes up with his heart pounding with ambition, dreaming of the idea, "Does she love me? . . ." One day he receives a declaration of love from her.

"And here I, a poor peasant, get a declaration of love from a great lady!"

Mathilde, high-minded and upright, is carried away for the first time by passionate emotion. She is a La Mole; she stems from the great La Mole of the sixteenth century. She is a woman of the Renaissance, or at least would like to be one. She likes to think that Julien himself is a great character. She gives him a rendezvous, at night, in her room. He can only reach it by putting a ladder to Mathilde's window. He will undoubtedly be caught, perhaps killed by the Marquis or his people. But a Stendhal hero never yields to fear, and Julien becomes Mathilde's lover.

There is no real love between these two beings. Mathilde makes an effort to thee-and-thou him. He has re-

136

course to his memory and recites several beautiful passages from *The New Héloïse*.

"This thee-and-thouing, shorn of a note of tenderness, gave Julien no pleasure. . . He was astonished at the absence of happiness. In vain he tried to induce it by resorting to reason. He saw himself esteemed by this proud young creature. With this reflection he was able to achieve the pleasure of self-esteem. It was not, to be sure, the heavenly bliss that he had sometimes experienced with Madame de Rênal. Great God, what a difference! There was nothing tender in his feelings from that first moment. It was the most intense joy of ambition, and Julien was above all ambitious."

Nor is Mathilde happy. She is shocked at his air of triumph.

"So he thinks he is my master. . . It is enough to make love hateful!"

Without being aware of it, the two lovers are for several days animated by the most intense hatred for each other. Then youth takes the upper hand and *pride yields*.

The Stendhalian doctrine requires that happiness then appear. Mathilde cuts her hair in sacrifice to Julien and shows the mad passion she feels for him. Soon the Marquis cannot but consent to the marriage. Unfortunately it occurs to him to ask the Rênals for information about

Julien. Madame de Rênal consults her confessor, who instructs her to tell the truth about Julien. The letter that the Marquis receives is such that the marriage does not take place. This provokes Julien to feel a hatred for Madame de Rênal which is all the more intense as by this action she has destroyed the image he had formed of her. For this is the one thing he does not forgive her. He goes to Verrières, enters the church where she is praying and, at the moment of the Elevation, fires a pistol at her. Madame de Rênal comes to see him in his prison and he realizes that he has never loved anyone but her. He dies on the guillotine. Mathilde, becoming more and more a woman of the Renaissance, has the fortitude to look squarely at Julien's cut-off head and to kiss it on the brow. Three days after Julien, Madame de Rênal dies embracing her children.

What is one to think of these two women? Even though he tends to regard both of them as women in whom modesty is overcome by the strength of their passions, Stendhal obviously prefers Madame de Rênal. He admires Mathilde's character; he does not love her. He considers that Mathilde's love is too long mixed with pride.

There is only one form of pride that Stendhal can pardon in women, and this is jealousy. Madame de

Rênal herself is pricked by it when she believes Julien loves her chamber maid.

"A woman of generous character," says Stendhal, "will sacrifice her life a thousand times for her lover and will break with him forever over a quarrel of pride about an open or a closed door. That is their point of honor."

This weakness is due to the fact that women have no opportunity to exercise pride in matters that men consider important: affairs of state, feats of arms. "They feel pride in their souls and they perceive that they can make their pride felt only in little things," and so they attach infinite importance to these little things.

But in Mathilde as in Madame de Rênal, Stendhal praises a *courage* even greater than Julien's, which is remarkable enough. Madame de Rênal does not hesitate to receive Julien even though she knows her husband has been warned, nor to go and see him in prison after the attempted murder. Mathilde is heroic to the point of defiance. Stendhal believes (and I think he is right) that the courage of a woman in love is greater than that of men.

"I remember having come upon the following sentence in a book of history:

" 'All the men lost their heads; it was one of those moments when women assume unquestionable superiority over them.'

"I have seen some on occasion who were superior to the bravest men. They need only a man to love. As they no longer feel except through him, the most atrocious direct and personal danger becomes for them like a rose to be plucked in his presence. As for moral courage, so much superior to the other, the firmness of a woman who resists her love is the most admirable thing that can exist on earth. All possible other marks of courage are trifles compared to a thing so much against nature, and so painful. . . One misfortune of women is that the test of this courage always remains secret and can almost never be divulged. A greater misfortune is that it is always exercised against their happiness. I believe that if Madame de Clèves had attained old age, which is a time when one judges life, and the joys of pride appear in all their wretchedness, she would have wished she had lived like Madame de La Fayette. . ."

Rather than the courage "against love" of the Princesse de Clèves, Stendhal likes to encounter in women the contempt for all that is not love. It is this contempt that constitutes what he calls "a sublime soul". For a woman and even for a man, he wants the sentiments alone to be important. *All else is vanity. Madame de Rênal and Mathilde are both, as he sees them, saved by the strength of their emotions.*

In the *Charterhouse of Parma,* the Duchesse San-severina and Clelia Conti are contrasted in the same way as are Mathilde de la Mole and Madame de Rênal.

Like Mathilde, the duchess is a woman of the Renaissance (and we know in fact that in order to write the *Charterhouse* Stendhal transported into the nineteenth century the history of the Farnese family); she is capable of assassination in order to save Fabrice, her nephew, whom she loves. Stendhal is fascinated by her because she sacrifices power and riches to her emotions without regrets, because she has a great deal of intelligence and no prudence.

"Young, brilliant, light as a bird, her beauty is her least charm. Where else can you find such a soul, ever sincere, that delivers itself wholly to the impression of the moment?"

A woman entirely of impulse, whose conduct is unpredictable, even to herself.

As for Clelia Conti, she is the most perfect example of *crystallization,* for Fabrice, who loves her madly, scarcely knows her. What does he know of her? He first catches a glimpse of her on a road, and he is struck by her young beauty.

"What profound thoughts beneath that brow!" he says to himself. "She could love!"

By chance she falls for a moment into his arms. On

this feeble armature of memories he crystallizes. Nothing is finer than the pages in which Fabrice is shown in the Parma prison, expecting death at any moment, and yet divinely happy because from his window he can perceive Clelia. Again, what does he know of her? Almost nothing. She is not very intelligent; when she has sworn not to see Fabrice again, she keeps her oath because she is superstitious; she thinks she is keeping it when she receives Fabrice in the dark. But what does intelligence matter? Clelia is beautiful and, as Fabrice had guessed, she can love. That convex brow, that passionate silence are unfailing signs to those who know women. Besides, she saves the mystery. This is enough. But in any case, re-read *The Charterhouse*. There is no finer book.

5. THE UNCOMPLETED NOVELS

Of the heroine of *Lucien Leuwen*, Madame de Chasteller, it is difficult to speak, for her character is merely sketched. But there is, in Stendhal's work, another very curious type of woman: this is the heroine of the uncompleted novel entitled *Lamiel*.

Lamiel is that startling character, a woman entirely devoid of hypocrisy. All the other women Stendhal has painted are restrained either by an extreme modesty (like

Madame de Rênal and Clelia Conti), or by a long habituation to society and a respect for the conventions which
it imposes (like Mathilde de la Mole and the Duchesse
Sanseverina). But Lamiel is a woman of the people; she
does not believe in the conventions of society; like Julien
Sorel, whom she exactly parallels, she finds herself involved in this society that she despises because she becomes a reader to a duchess, as Julien is secretary to Monsieur de la Mole. Like Julien Sorel, she admires only
"great souls," and by this she means beings without fear,
even though they be criminals. As a mere child, Lamiel
read stories of thieves and assassins. She admires "Monsieur Cartouche and Monsieur Mandrin" for their great
deeds. Her cynicism is fed by a diabolical little hunch-
back, Doctor Sansfin:

"Old women," he tells her, "preach virtue to young
girls, but several of those old women in their youth had
the easy morals that prevailed in France before the reign
of Napoleon and in their hearts they must laugh at the
atrocious restraints that they impose on girls who are sixteen in 1829. So there is a double advantage in listening to the advice of nature and in following all its caprices.
First you give yourself pleasure, which is the only object
for which the human race has been placed here below.
In the second place, the soul fortified by pleasure, which
is its true element, has the courage to omit none of the

little comedies necessary for a girl to obtain a position from the old women in good standing in the villages."

To put the Doctor's lessons into practice, Lamiel chooses the young Duke as a subject, and seduces him even more cynically than Julien Sorel had seduced Mathilde. He has never met a woman so bold, nor so original; he is mad about her. She proposes that she run away with him. Not that she loves him:

"God deliver me from lovers! I prefer my freedom to anything else! . . ."

When Lamiel tries to live freely, to travel alone, she realizes that this is difficult for a pretty woman, because she is constantly exposed to men's advances. A timid boy, who is an apothecary, suggests to her a means of overcoming this:

"Pharmacists," he tells her, "grind up holly-leaves; you know—those leaves that have thorns on their edges and are such a pretty green . . . You make a colored paste with them. By rubbing it into her cheek a woman can look as if she had a frightful green scurf. Your coquetry, Mademoiselle, will have to choose between love and tranquillity. Tomorrow morning, before getting into the coach, it is in your power to make yourself almost as ugly as me."

Lamiel laughs heartily at the recipe.

"This apothecary," she says, "is sensible and he has something to say."

The following day she uses the holly-paste and finds herself thus freed of men. This episode is a hard and useful lesson to women.

When she arrives in Paris, Lamiel becomes a fashionable woman. But in the midst of the dinners that degenerate into orgies, it becomes evident that licentiousness has no attraction for her. She preserves a tone of refined politeness that captivates people. Passionate love has disappointed her; love-as-pleasure is indifferent to her . . . And here ends the written part of the novel. But in the plan that Stendhal has left, we see that Lamiel meets a thief:

" 'Who are you?'

" 'I make war on society which makes war on me. I read Corneille and Molière. I have too much education to work with my hands and earn three hundred francs for ten hours of work.' "

Although he is being sought by the police, he proudly takes her to the theatre. This audacity causes her to fall madly in love. In the end, out of love for this Valbayre, she joins a gang of thieves. When Valbayre is condemned to the galleys, Lamiel sets fire to the Hall of Justice to avenge him. In the wreckage are found some half-calcinated bones: they are Lamiel's.

Stendhal would certainly have enjoyed intensely writing this story and it is too bad he was unable to finish it. *Few novels have been written on the cynical woman because men fear her type and because they even have difficulty in conceiving her.* One shudders to think what would be the power in society of a Lamiel—very beautiful, intelligent, courageous even unto death, without moral principles and without pride. And so men have seen to it that *Lamiel* should scarcely exist. This novel has few readers.

6.

Such were the imaginary heroines created by this man who held such passionate feelings for women and who, in real women, already loved imaginary heroines. "A writer," as Paul Valéry has said, "compensates as best he can for any injustice of fate." Never was this remark more applicable than to the case of Stendhal. Through his novels he offered himself these women, so beautiful, so intelligent, so perfectly capable of love, whom he had not chanced to encounter in life.

If now we try to determine what is the place of Stendhal in this history of love as seen through the French novel whose broad lines we are sketching it must be said, I think, that love in Stendhal is as passionate, as "romantic" as in Rousseau, but that his modes of expression are much less emphatic. It is, I believe, one of the reasons why *The Charterhouse of Parma* has more readers in 1943 than it had in 1840, whereas *The New Héloïse*, once triumphant, is now practically ignored.

Men and women, almost without exception, and in all times, suffer from having to stilt their phrases and their feelings. They have been stuffed with the language of false virtue and of false passion to the point of nausea. "I am so fond of naturalness," says Stendhal, "that sometimes I stop in the street to watch a dog gnaw a bone." We all like naturalness, especially in love, and we seldom meet it. This is why we are so grateful to Stendhal for having brought us its image. That a lover should dare to say, "I was timid, I was unhappy, and because of this I was divinely happy"—so much simplicity moves us.

"Dear reader, do not spend your life hating and being afraid." This is Stendhal's key-phrase. A negative counsel, but one which makes it easy to reconstruct the positive counsel. "Dear reader, spend your life loving with passion what deserves to be loved. Dear reader, never be afraid of the strength of your feelings." Stendhal all his life passionately loved Cimarosa, Mozart, Byron, and a few imaginary great souls. He had a horror of "Important People" who have as their goal in life a satisfied ambition and not happy love. By this he remains, for those who are worthy, a good master to love and to meditate.

Is he, like Rousseau, the incarnation of an epoch of French life? He is, indeed, a man of the eighteenth century and a soldier of Napoleon. Like the nobility after the *Fronde,* the half-pay soldiers after the Restoration were a generation of "tamed lions." But if, in Stendhal, the features of the heroes of his time are present, he shows himself singularly free of their jargon. Bonaparte the lover wrote like Rousseau; Stendhal the lover tried to write with the dry preciseness of the Napoleonic Code. A style that is naked, stripped of adornments, and that is molded to things, does not age. It is hardly possible any longer to love as Saint-Preux loved; one could still love like Fabrice, if one met a Clelia.

FIVE

IDEAL AND SENSUAL LOVE

Some Heroines of Balzac

HAT THE WORK of Balzac holds a supremely important place in the history of the sentiments of love in France is obvious. But this place is so great and the variety of feminine types created by Balzac so astonishing that it would be impossible to treat the subject adequately within the limits of a single study. With Balzac we shall do better by confronting a problem which our preceding surveys have already broached, that of the relations between the novel-heroines and the real women observed by novelists. This is a difficult problem. The transmutations that occur in a creative brain are strange and complex. But sometimes the author has set down for us some of the secret formulae of his alchemy. Marcel Proust's *Notebooks* enable us to follow the transformation of Laura Heyman into Odette de Crécy. They render intelligible the curious alloying which lends to Oriane de Guermantes the beauty of the Comtesse Greffulhe, the wisdom of Madame Strauss, and the wit of the Comtesse de Chévigné. The successive manuscripts of Anatole France's *The Red Lily* show how Madame Arman de Caillavet—with her toque of violets, her passionate fondness for Italy, her despotic father, and her arrow of diamonds—was transposed into Thérèse Martin-Bellème. In the case of Balzac, we know that George Sand and Marie d'Agoult served as models for the heroines of *Beatrix*. Naturally it would not be literally exact to say that Madame de Mortsauf, in *The Lily in the Valley*, is Madame de Berny, nor that the *Duchesse de Langeais* is the Duchesse de Castries. But it is true that if Balzac had not known Madame de Berny and the Duchesse de Castries these two novels could not have been written, and in the case of the greatest of all novelists it seems interesting to confront real life and novelized life, women of flesh and women of words.

1. THE MAN

When we read the stories of childhood in *The Lily in the Valley* or in *Louis Lambert,* which Balzac assures us are a reflection of his own childhood, we observe that these reflect suffering. Yet Balzac did not have reasons for being an unhappy child comparable to those of Dickens: shame and poverty. When he was born, in 1799, his father, who was Food Commissioner of the Military Division of Tours, was a respectable and comfortably situated man. But he had married a woman thirty-two years younger than himself, Laure Sallembier, and it is to her, it seems, that the wretchedness of Balzac as a child must be attributed.

Madame Balzac was extremely pretty, with the face of a soubrette in a Molière or a Marivaux comedy, refined, unusually well educated, with a passion for occult sciences. But she was a coquette, with a hardness at the core, and she gave ground for gossip to the neighbors, who did not attribute the paternity of her second son, Henri, to her husband. Perhaps she reserved for this younger son, a love-child, a great share of her tenderness; it is a fact that she always sought to get her other son, Honoré, away from the house. The latter, however, did not hold this against her; he felt affection, even filial love, for her, but he never ceased to be afraid of her. As a mature man, he could never come near her without trembling, and many times in his works he speaks of the need of feminine protection that those feel all their lives who have been deprived of a true maternal love.

From his eighth to his fourteenth years Balzac was an interne student with the Oratorians of Vendôme. He tells us, in *Louis Lambert*, that he there became "the least active, the laziest, the most contemplative schoolboy in the youngsters' division, and yet the most often punished." In Vendôme he read a great deal, got what he calls "a congestion of ideas" and became—he who had been a big, jovial boy—a child so pale and thin that in 1813 a letter from the Director begged his family to take him back and care for him. He recovered quickly, completed his studies in Tours, then in Paris, where his father had received an appointment, and entered a solicitor's office at the age of seventeen.

We have a portrait of him by Deveria, drawn at about this time. The head is well-shaped, the eyes bright and tender, the expression frank and wholesome. We know that he then displayed an exuberant gayety and a boisterous verve. Yet he did not consider himself a happy person. His favorite motto was, *"Fuge, late, tace*—flee, hide yourself, keep silent." Between this desire to keep in the shadow and his solar gayety the contradiction is only apparent. Verve and loud laughter, in certain beings, are violent states that more or less adequately mask the emotions. Balzac was possessed of burning passions. What did he want? To be famous and to be loved . . . Now he was an obscure notary's clerk, his father did not give him a sou, and the women of Paris, who struck him as so beautiful, did not look at him.

To his favorite sister Laura, who like so many sisters of men of genius was for him a *confidante* and an ally, he writes, "And this mill-stone rotation they call living! If there were only someone to give a touch of warmth to this cold existence! I have not yet produced the flowers of life and I am in the only season when they bloom! Of what use to me is fortune and its enjoyment at the age of sixty, when all you can do is be present to watch others live, when you have only to pay for your seat and it is no longer necessary to wear actors' clothes? An old man is a fellow who has had his dinner and who watches the others come eat theirs. Well, my platter is empty, it is not golden, the tablecloth is dull, the dishes insipid. I am hungry and there is nothing to feed my appetite. What do I need? . . . Ortolans—for I have only two passions —love and glory—and nothing is yet satisfied, nothing ever will be . . ." This is the stereotyped complaint of adolescents.

When he reached the age of twenty, his father made

him a proposal: Honoré could marry the daughter of a great notary and later become the head of the office. Monsieur Balzac found this solution all the more attractive as he himself had just been retired and was going to live henceforth in the country. Honoré answered that since his childhood his dream had been to write and that he did not want to be a notary. The family became indignant; his brilliant and cruel mother made fun of him; only Laura took his side. He had an iron will; he won out. His father (over Madame Balzac's protests) allowed him a grace period of two years, during which the young man would receive fifteen hundred francs a year. After this trial period, if he had not given proof of his genius, he would have to return to the ranks. Here he is, then, established in a mansard attic on Rue Lesdiguières, working like a convict and challenging Paris, as his hero Rastignac was to do later. One may recall the last lines of *Old Goriot*:

"Rastignac, left to himself, took a few steps toward the upper end of the cemetery and saw Paris lying tortuously along the two banks of the Seine, where the lights were beginning to gleam. His eyes fastened almost avidly to the part of it stretching between the Place Vendôme and the Dome of the Invalides, where lived the high society to which it had been his dream to be admitted. Over this humming hive he cast a glance that seemed in anticipation to suck the store of honey, and uttered these grandiose words, "And now we two can fight it out! . . ."

But in 1821 Balzac was hardly thinking of composing novels on the manners of his time. This was an unknown *genre*. Known were the personal, analytic novel in the manner of Benjamin Constant's *Adolphe;* the novel in the form of letters of the type of *Delphine,* by Madame de Staël, and *The New Héloïse;* the historical novel *à la* Walter Scott. No one, save perhaps Henri Beyle, then wholly unknown, thought of describing an epoch, which yet was the most romantic the world had ever known: the dramas of the Revolution, of the Empire, and of the Restoration. After an unsuccessful attempt at tragedy Balzac, in his attic, tried his hand under assumed names at popular novels—far-fetched and full of terror, which (though less well done) were reminiscent of *Bug Jargal* and *Han d'Islande* that Victor Hugo was composing at about the same time.

The young Honoré de Balzac had verve, gifts, perhaps genius, but he lacked subjects and material. He had to learn about life and love. At this point the first woman in his life appears.

2. *LA DILECTA*

In Villeparisis, to which Monsieur de Balzac the elder had retired (the "de" had been added by the family at the time of Laura's marriage to Monsieur de Surville), lived a Madame de Berny who, by a curious coincidence, bore the name of *Laura*, like Balzac's mother and like his sister. A woman of forty-five, the daughter of a German musician who had been attached to Marie-Antoinette, the goddaughter of the Queen, the wife of a man of rank who was capricious and cantankerous, by whom she had had nine children, she was not beautiful (her nose, in particular, was unenviably conspicuous). But she preserved an air of finesse—supple, with a suggestion of languor, even of voluptuousness about her. Perhaps it was from her German father that she had acquired a caressing softness, to which the Court of France had fortunately added wit, gayety and a touch of cynicism.

Like most adolescents, Balzac had for a long time been in love, without knowing with whom. A great reader of *The New Héloïse* and the *Confessions*, he was looking for a Madame de Warens.

"This is how I am and how I will always be—excessively timid, madly in love, and chaste to the point of not daring to say, 'I love.' I admit that there is nothing I resemble less than a lover; I have neither the air nor the manners of a lover; I have neither grace nor boldness; nothing aggressive; in a word, I am like certain girls who appear awkward, stupid, timid, gentle, and who hide under this veil a fire which, once it has burst through the ashes that cover it, will consume the heart, and the house, and everything . . . Yet I shall never describe my character better than has already been done by a great man. Re-read the *Confessions* and you will find it throughout . . ."

This is an extremely revealing text, which shows us that we must not attach too much importance to Balzac's blustering side.

Deprived of maternal love, drawn toward the mature woman who could bring him knowledge of the world, he wrote to this forty-year-old mother of a family ardent letters.

"I expect from you neither love, nor astonishment, nor mockery, nor disdain, even less contempt. But I have always suspected that there was in the heart of every woman a feeling that lies on the confines of tenderness and friendship: it is the compassion, the generous pity that holds out a hand to madmen as to the unhappy . . . Adieu, Madame, adieu, and permit me, instead of the banal phrases with which one usually concludes, to deposit here, in this place, my whole soul, an unsullied, irreproachable soul, which I make bold to offer you as one of the purest gifts that anyone could receive. Adieu . . ."

Madame de Berny was probably surprised, but she answered, which is always imprudent—and perhaps she wanted to be imprudent. Immediately the young Balzac became more enterprising.

"The first time I saw you, my senses were stirred and my imagination kindled to the point of believing you to be perfect . . . So your forty-five years do not exist for me, or if I am aware of them for a moment I regard them as a proof of the strength of my passion, since you seem to think they ought to break its charm . . . Your age, which would make you ridiculous to me if really I did not love you, is on the contrary a bond, something pungent which by its oddness and its contrast with usual ideas, attaches me . . ."

There were conversations, hours spent reading together, meetings at night in the garden, the husband's absences, and in a few weeks this adventure reached its normal climax:

"Oh Laura, it is in the middle of a night full of you, in the bosom of its silence and pursued by the memory of your mad kisses that I write you—and what ideas can I possibly have? You have carried them all away. Yes, my entire soul has become attached to yours and you will walk henceforth only with me . . . Oh! I am surrounded by a tenderly enchanting and magic wonder; I see only the bench, I feel only your soft pressure, and the flowers that are before me, all withered though they are, preserve an intoxicating fragrance . . . You betray fears and you express them in a tone that rends my heart. Alas! I am sure now of what I swore to you, for your kisses have changed nothing . . . Oh! yes, I am changed, I love you to the point of madness!"

So far there is nothing that is not quite ordinary. The sequel is more highly seasoned. Madame de Berny, having lived at the Court, having known through her mother (who had been lady-in-waiting to the Queen) a thousand stories of the Old Régime, having lived through the Revolution under romantic circumstances and kept many aristocratic friends in the society of the Restoration, could teach Balzac many a thing on life and on society. Now it happened that this young man had a voracious, universal curiosity. Everything interested him: business, politics, women's dresses, furniture, houses, and especially "the seamy side of contemporary history," the secret side of History. Madame de Berny, on all these subjects, was rich in memories. How many novels she must have told him between kisses, on the garden bench!

She gave him not only subjects but the audacity to treat them. At this moment he needed, more than anything

else, tenderness, admiration, a woman who believed un-
reservedly in his genius. Laura de Berny was this woman
and she made Balzac conscious of his power. "At the
beginning of my life," he writes after her death, "she was
a true mother . . . *Mon Dieu,* I have not a *soul* that
knows me; there was only one . . ."

The style of Madame de Berny, whose letters we have,
was not very good. More exactly, it was banal, and resembled all the cooings of women in love, which are vocal
exercises rather than phrases. But the literary influence
on Balzac of the first woman who knew him well was
none the less excellent. It was she who gave him, through
her stories, the precious and new idea of composing on his
own time novels similar to those of Walter Scott. On her
advice he made a stay in Fougères, at General de Pom-
mereul's, which gave him the material he needed to write
The Chouans. Had it not been for her we should perhaps
not have had our Balzac. For there are geniuses who die
without having expressed themselves. But after her came
others, who completed her work.

3. *THE OTHERS*

Balzac's second inspirer was the Duchesse d'Abrantès,
Madame Junot, whose name also was *Laura,* and to whom
he had perhaps been attracted because of that fateful

name. Madame d'Abrantès was no younger than Madame de Berny; she had the voice of an old non-com, a horse-like profile. But for a Balzac she was prodigiously interesting, having known the Emperor Napoleon, been Metternich's mistress, and reigned at Junot's side in Spain and Portugal. To the *Human Comedy* she brought the Empire, as Madame de Berny had brought the Old Régime. It was a coalition ministry.

Two other women participated in this initiation of Balzac to life. Madame Zulma Carraud, a boarding-school friend of Laura Balzac de Surville, had married an instructing officer at Saint-Cyr. Of all Balzac's inspirers, she was the most discriminating. She was also the most inaccessible and never did he speak to her of love.

"I do not want," she wrote to him, "I have never wanted the charming friendship you offer to the women who in a thousand ways are better than I. I aspire to a more elevated sentiment. You must esteem me enough to put me in reserve, so to speak; and if something unforeseen should come and disturb your joy, if some disappointment should wound your heart, you can then appeal to me and you will see how I will respond to such a call."

She was faithful to this program and her whole correspondence with Balzac inspires the highest opinion of her character and her intelligence. Yet it seems that she brought him fewer useful elements of work than Laure de Berny, than Laure d'Abrantès or than a third Muse, the Marquise (later Duchesse) de Castries. The latter, *née* Maille, had written to Balzac in 1831, under the name of an imaginary Englishwoman, as for that matter she had written to Sainte-Beuve after he had published *Volupté,* and as she was subsequently to write to many other novelists. He answered her letter. She ended by giving him her real name, and received him in the boudoir where she had spent her life, almost always recumbent, ever since she had been injured in a hunting accident. Illness is for women both a defense and a charm. The burning and naive Balzac fell head over heels in love. This was an unlucky stroke. Madame de Castries was a coquette, happy to arouse desires, firmly resolved not to satisfy them. Like all wealthy women she cost him plenty of money, for in order to please her he wanted to have a tilbury, two servants, two horses, a loge at the Opera, and to live on the scale of a man of fashion.

He incurred many debts, declared his love and obtained nothing. Madame de Castries made fun of him, forced him to travel, called him to Aix-les-Bains where she was taking the waters, and yielded him not a whit more in Savoy than she had in Paris.

"I have to traipse all the way to Aix," he wrote to Zulma Carraud, "run after someone who makes fun of me . . . One of those aristocratic women you hate; one of those angelic beauties to whom one attributes a fine soul; the true Duchess, very disdainful, very loving, discriminating, witty, coquettish—she is like nothing I have ever known!—a phenomenon who says she loves me, and then vanishes, who wants to keep me stowed away in a palace in Venice . . . and who wants me to write only for her . . . One of those women whom you must worship on your knees when they want you to, and whom it is such a pleasure to conquer; the woman of dreams! . . . Ah! I would be better off in Angoulème, at the Poudrerie, nice and quiet, listening to the mills rattle and stuffing myself with truffles, laughing and talking . . . than wasting my time and my life . . ."

One can imagine how much all these intrigues worried Madame de Berny.

"A deadly fear sometimes makes my heart leap," she would write to Balzac. "I think that if a certain lady should write you asking you to come to her you would be good enough to go! Didn't another lady (Madame d'Abrantès) make you come back all the way from Tours to Versailles to console her for troubles which her egoism made her exaggerate to you? Here the circumstance is much more serious, and unfortunately your vanity is always awake and active and has all the more hold over you since you have no idea of its strength. However, my dearly beloved, friend, son of love, if you will, do listen to reason . . ."

He listened to her all the more readily as he was coming to hate the Duchesse de Castries. A great worker is always saved from flirts in the end by the time they make him lose. Moreover, the perspicacity of a woman in love is very adept at tearing other women apart. Read Madame de Berny on the subject of the Duchesse de Castries' prose:

"My darling, what a fabric of brazen lies! of sanctimoniousness! of vanity! of exaggerations of every sort! Ah! my pet, it is your good angel that has delivered you from the misfortune of belonging to such a woman . . ."

It is a curious phenomenon that Madame de Berny, who herself wrote in such bad taste, gave Balzac the best kind of literary advice. He needed to have close to him a woman-genius—but for whom, he used to say, he would go "slightly mad." When *Louis Lambert* was in proof he asked *la Dilecta* for her criticisms; they were everything they should have been. Madame de Berny made him feel the danger there was in depicting a "superior spirit" and in saying of his hero "that he has developed thought to its vastest expression." She urged Balzac not to brag, as he usually did.

"Let the crowd see you, my darling, from all sides because of the height you have reached, but don't yell to them to admire you . . ."

And so it is right that he should have dedicated *Louis Lambert* to her: "*Et nunc et semper Dilectae dedicatum* . . . Both now and always dedicated to the beloved . . ." It is right also that he should have written in *The Duchesse de Langeais*: "It is only a woman's last love that can satisfy a man's first."

Unfortunately, in 1832 Madame de Berny is fifty-six years old, and, however tender Balzac tries to be toward her, he shows a little weariness.

"Since I have had ideas and feelings," Balzac writes, "I have belonged wholly to love, and the first person I met was an accomplished heroine, an angelic heart, the most discriminating spirit. Diabolical Nature had added to this a fatal *but!* . . . BUT she was twenty-two years older than I, so that if the ideal was morally surpassed, the material, which counts for a good deal, imposed impassable limits . . . I lacked one-half of everything."

A mistress of fifty-two cannot but be indulgent: she can open her arms when her unhappy lover comes and weeps to her over the humiliations which another woman has inflicted on him. It was to Madame de Berny that Balzac confessed his love's labors lost with Madame de Castries, and then another adventure with a beautiful Polish woman, Madame Hanska (who much later was to become Madame de Balzac). To the latter, whom he called *l'Etrangère*, he wrote:

"Tomorrow, if you wished it, I would break my pen; tomorrow no woman would hear my voice again . . . I would only ask mercy for *la Dilecta*, who is my mother; she will soon be fifty-eight; you would not be jealous of her, you who are so young!"

It is an essential trait of Balzac's genius that he was engendered, nourished, raised by women. Before him, novelists had hardly spoken of women except as men. Madame de Clèves, Julia, are less real women than women such as men would like them to be. Even the women novelists, Madame de La Fayette, Madame de Staël, sacrificed their profound knowledge of their sex to the exigencies of the male readers who ask for lovely falsehoods. But the heroines of Balzac, physiologically and emotionally, are women. Read the *Memoirs of Two Young Married Women, The Woman of Thirty, Cousin Bette,* and especially the *Secrets of the Princesse Cadignan*—every sincere woman will admit that these cruel portraits are true.

Because he loved women older than himself, Balzac prolonged the age of love in fiction. The Woman of Thirty is born to the novel thanks to him, even though he did not dare to depict his own case—deeply moving as it is—to its conclusion, nor the death of the old woman whom one has once loved. In 1834 began the illness which was to be Madame de Berny's last.

"She carries friendship to the point of concealing her sufferings from me; she wants to be well because of me. *Grand Dieu!* How she has changed in the last two months! I was horror-stricken."

When she was dead:

"I went back to my labors this morning, in obedience to the last words Madame de Berny wrote me . . . She had only one criticism to make of *The Lily in the Valley,* and it was in this connection that she wrote, 'I can now die; I am sure you will wear on your brow the crown I have always wished to see there. The *Lily* is a sublime work, without flaw nor rift. Only—the death of Madame de Mortsauf does not require her horrible regrets; they spoil the beautiful letter she writes.' So, today, I have piously cut out the hundred lines which, according to many people, detracted from this creation. I have not regretted a single one of them and each time my pen passed over one, never was a man's heart more strongly moved. I thought I saw that great and sublime woman, that angel of friendship, before me, smiling at me as she would smile when I made use of that force which is so rare, which consists of cutting off one of one's members and feeling neither pain nor regret, of correcting and conquering oneself!"

Here we discover Balzac at his best. "That great and sublime woman . . ." One of Balzac's superiorities over most other novelists is that he was never afraid to depict sublime creatures, nor for that matter to portray monsters. If *The Human Comedy* is illuminated, here and there, by a few fine-souled characters, this is due in large part to Laure de Berny. And of this *The Lily in the Valley* is the most striking example.

4. FROM REALITY TO FICTION

Balzac had immediate reasons for writing *The Lily in the Valley*. The first was the fatal illness of Madame de Berny, a threat that inspired Balzac with the desire to erect a literary monument to his friend that would be worthy of her and that she might see before she died. The second, less noble, but also less compelling, was the publication by Sainte-Beuve of his novel, *Volupté*.

Balzac and Sainte-Beuve did not like each other. And how could they have liked each other? Sainte-Beuve, a man of taste, was shocked by what he regarded as Balzac's vulgarity; Balzac, a man of fire, was exasperated by Sainte-Beuve's style, which he considered wavering and soft. Moreover, Sainte-Beuve, as a critic, had treated Balzac very badly, so that the latter was delighted when

Sainte-Beuve, turning novelist, laid himself open to criticism. There was in Sainte-Beuve something of a frustrated creator; criticism seemed to him a last resort. He was wrong, for he made criticism creative, but such was his feeling; he desired passionately to be a poet and a novelist. So he had undertaken to write a novel, inspired by his love of Madame Victor Hugo. *Volupté* was the story of the chaste love of a timid and passionate youth for a virtuous woman; of secret sensual pleasures to which the hero resorts to appease his senses; and finally of a conversion. There were some fine things about the novel, for Sainte-Beuve's discrimination could not wholly fail to make itself felt; but it was too literary, saturated with Chateaubriand, and lifeless. In reading it, Balzac must have triumphed and said to himself, "Why, this is the beginning of my adventure with Laura, transposed into a platonic *liaison*. A fine subject. I can do it over again, a hundred times better than Sainte-Beuve." Whence *The Lily in the Valley*.

The subject is very simple, but it is the ideal subject for a novel—the progressive discovery of love by an adolescent. Félix de Vandenesse, belonging to a noble family of Touraine, has had a difficult childhood (Balzac's). He knows nothing of women.

"I was growing out of an adolescence retarded by my labors into a maturity which was belatedly pushing forth its green shoots. No young man was better prepared than I to feel and to love. If you are to appreciate what is to follow you must imagine yourself carried back to that lovely age when your lips were virgin of lies, when your eyes looked frankly and fearlessly at the world, though veiled by eyelids weighted by the timidities that conflict with desire, when your mind did not give ground to the jesuitism of society, when the cowardice of your heart equalled in violence the generosity of your first impulse."

One day, in his province of Touraine, at the age of twenty, he attends his first ball and finds himself seated beside an unknown woman, so beautiful that without knowing what he is doing, Félix kisses her bare shoulder. She utters a piercing cry, turns round and says, "Monsieur!" and walks off with the stateliness of a queen.

Who is she? Félix does not dare ask, looks for her everywhere in Touraine. One day he discovers a ravishing valley, a magnificent emerald bowl at the bottom of which the river Indre indolently winds its coils.

"If this woman lives anywhere in the world," thinks Félix, "this is the place."

He is not mistaken, and it is in the little château of Clochegourde that Madame de Mortsauf lives. He is introduced there by a neighbor. She has two sick children, a prematurely aged husband, who is a restless, jealous, odious character. But it has never occurred to her that she could do anything else in her life than devote herself to her family. Yet she suffers, and Félix who also knows moral anguish understands her sufferings. As she is pure, she does not take umbrage when she sees him come to call. Besides, he has won over the Comte de Mortsauf by his willingness to take lessons in backgammon, and in agriculture.

But the moment Félix broaches the subject of love, Madame de Mortsauf stops him:

"That is the one thing you mustn't do. If you don't understand, I shall have to ask you never to come again."

He accepts the condition, and is content occasionally to brush against her dress, kiss her hand . . .

"When words failed, silence faithfully served our souls which, so to speak, entered each into the other without obstacle, but without being invited by a kiss: both savoring the charms of a pensive torpor, they launched upon the waves of the same revery, plunged together into the river, emerged refreshed like two nymphs as perfectly united as jealousy could wish, but without any terrestrial bond. We would enter into a bottomless pit, return to the surface empty-handed, asking each other with a glance, 'Will we ever have just a day that we can call our own among so many days?' "

Then Félix enters into political life, guided by Madame de Mortsauf's wisdom, as Balzac had been by that

of Madame de Berny; he obtains a confidential post under
Louis XVIII.

"Madame de Mortsauf had seen the thing clearly. I
owed her everything: power and riches, happiness and
knowledge; she guided and encouraged me, purified my
heart and gave to my will that unity without which the
forces of youth are uselessly spent."

In Paris he meets a beautiful Englishwoman, Lady
Arabelle Dudley, who tries to win him because she feels
him to be bound to another. Resistance sharpens their
passions.

"Laughingly she would make the humblest offers,
promise a limitless discretion, or else again merely ask to
be allowed to love me. One day, appealing to all the
waverings of my over-scrupulous conscience and the
frenzied desires of my youth, she said to me:

"'I shall always be your friend, and your mistress
whenever you want me.'

"At last she plotted to use my very integrity to bring
about my undoing; she won over my valet, and after an
evening when she had appeared so beautiful that she was
sure she had excited my desires, I found her in my apart-
ment."

From that moment Félix de Vandenesse is torn between Lady Dudley and Henriette de Mortsauf, as Balzac must have been between the aging Madame de Berny

and some younger mistress. Madame de Mortsauf dies of grief, and on the brink of eternity at last finds strength to confess her love.

"Farewell, dear child of my heart! This is the quite lucid farewell, still full of life, the farewell of a soul into which you have poured joys too great to allow you the least remorse over the catastrophe they have brought; I use this word, believing that you love me, for I am nearing my final rest, immolated to duty, and I tremble, not without regret . . ."

Such is this novel, which some consider ridiculous because the language of love it employs has a somewhat too noble cast. But this is how Laure de Berny spoke, who was none the less a woman very authentically in love. Was it then *her* novel? We know that it was not, that she was infinitely less lily-like than Madame de Mortsauf, that there was no Lady Dudley in Balzac's life. Yet she gave to the book that inner, intimate impulse without which a book is merely a book. The emotion of the adolescent who loves for the first time, the emotion of the man who, not without a sense of guilt, witnesses the death of the first woman he has loved, this is what Balzac found in his memories, and this is what makes *The Lily in the Valley* a "great and sublime" book. The novelist does not copy real women, but he owes to them the depth of feeling, the breath of life that animates the

173

creatures born of his imagination. Now read *The Du-chesse de Langeais* and you will see how he there trans-poses the coquetries of Madame de Castries, and the legitimate furies they aroused in Balzac.

5.

Because intelligent women had guided him, and be-cause he had been willing to be guided by them, Balzac created heroines more carnally feminine than his prede-cessors had done. To all appearances a few women played a great role in his emotional life. In fact they played such a role only to the extent to which they brought him elements for his work. "Now," he said one day, "we must look above the belt." He did see much higher than this, but he also knew what lies below the belt, and such was his duty as a novelist.

SIX

ESCAPE IN LOVE

Madame Bovary

"I CALL CLASSIC that which is healthy, romantic that which is unhealthy," said Goethe. This is true in a sense, for the classic strives to impose measure and form upon his ideas, while the romantic abandons himself to "the sensual delight of disaster." Perhaps it would be better to designate as classic every artist who strives to represent reality as it is, and romantic every art that flees reality. This would mean that no artist is altogether a classic, nor altogether a romantic. Corneille has romantic aspects and his heroes are bigger than life; Hugo has classic traits and his *Things Seen* are admirably realistic. But it is certain that there are epochs, the great classic epochs, in which most of the writers strive to observe men objectively, and others, the romantic epochs, when artists seek to evade reality and to live a dream.

We have shown that in the eighteenth century the romantic escape sometimes assumed the form of exoticism, that is to say a flight into space (*Paul and Virginia*), sometimes the form of a return to natural and primitive life, that is to say a flight into time (the noble Savage). In the nineteenth century the forms of escape are different, but the need of flight remains the same because the society of the Restoration contains numerous elements of instability. It does not accept itself. Whence a new escape into the past with the love of the romantics for historic novels (*Notre Dame de Paris, Cinq-Mars*); escape into a newly discovered class with the popular romanticism of George Sand and the men of 1848; escape into the future with the illusions of a Renan or a Zola as to the world that science will create.

Classic style is sober. Because it is objective, it employs above all substantives and verbs. Romantic style is lyrical and subjective, because its object is within the writer. Toward the middle of the nineteenth century, Musset in the *Letters of Dupuis and Cotonet*, made fun of the romantic style.

"Romanticism," he said, "is simply the art of employing useless adjectives."

176

And he gave a *Portrait of Two Children* in a natural style and in a romantic style.

Natural style:

"No cares had wrinkled their brows, no intemperance had corrupted their blood. No unhappy passion had depraved their hearts. Day by day love, innocence and piety enhanced the beauty of their souls with ineffable grace in their features, their attitudes and their movements."

Romantic style:

"No premature cares had wrinkled their innocent brows, no intemperance had corrupted their young blood, no unhappy passion had depraved their childish hearts, which were as fresh as flowers just unfolding; day by day their candid love, their innocence at play, their gentle piety enhanced the serene beauty of their radiant souls with ineffable grace in their supple attitudes and their harmonious movements."

This parody of romanticism by a disciple of Byron is a sign of the times; it shows that the elite reacts to it with disgust, at least in its vulgar forms. This disgust is to grow. About 1850 the French public, disappointed in the monarchy and in the republic, in the lyrical drama and the historic novel, in the excesses of passion as in those of the revolution, was ready to enjoy a book that would burn what it had worshipped, just as the Spanish public had been ready, in the time of *Don Quixote,* to welcome a parody of the novels of chivalry. It may be said (and I believe it is Albert Thibaudet who was the first to say it) that Flaubert is the Cervantes of the French novel. Before analyzing *Madame Bovary,* let us see how life had prepared this novelist to become (apparently at least) a condemner of the romantic.

1. THE MAN

At the outset he was "a child of the century." The son of a great surgeon of Rouen, he was raised in a hospital and his first vision of the world was a *Danse Macabre.*

"The amphitheatre of the Hospital overlooked our garden; how many times, with my sisters, we climbed the trellis and, hanging among the vines, looked at the outstretched corpses! The sun beat down on them, the same flies that circled round us and on the flowers alighted on them, came back, buzzed . . ."

Flaubert remains marked by this sight. Later, to his mistress Louise Colet, he writes: "The sight of a naked woman causes me to meditate about her skeleton."

Very young, too, he glimpses the skeleton of human souls, I mean that ossified armature of vulgar ideas which exists beneath the surface of the most remarkable spirits, of which Flaubert was to make the *Dictionary of Ac-*

cepted *Ideas, Bouvard and Pécuchet,* and no doubt also
the character of Homais. Thibaudet has remarked that
the first letter in his *Correspondence,* a letter written at
the age of nine, begins with this sentence, "Dear friend,
you are right in observing that New Year's Day is stupid." Almost all the actions of men appear to him stupid.

"Stupidity creeps into my pores," he says; "dismal gro-
tesqueness exerts an unbelievable charm upon me. It cor-
responds to an intimate need in my nature, which is
buffoonishly bitter. It does not make me laugh, but dream
endlessly. I feel it so well wherever it is to be found, as
well as in myself. This is why I love to analyze it; it is
a study that amuses me."

Flaubert's life is a long revolt against universal stupidity, a violent revolt. Flaubert was born *h'*indignant
(and he always writes the word with an aspirate *h,* to
accentuate its importance), indignant and exasperated
by those men "whose lives are filled by two passions: to
make their fortune and to live for themselves; that is to
say to constrict their souls between their shops and their
digestions." Flaubert's vice, his masochism, is that even
while hating bourgeois stupidity, he begins when he is
still very young, to depict it. His friends and he invented
a type of obstreperous Gaudissart (the hero of Balzac's
The Illustrious Gaudissart): Le Garçon, a kind of "ro-

mantic Guignol" whose role each of them would play by turn in the course of their walks about Rouen.

But this adolescent is as enthusiastic over beauty as he is revolted by baseness:

"Oh, how much better I love pure poetry, the cries of the soul, sudden outpourings, deep sighs, thoughts that come from the heart!"

His great literary admirations go to Hugo, Rabelais, Shakespeare, Byron and Rousseau's *Confessions;* Hugo above all, whom he loves passionately. When, one day, he is able to pay Victor Hugo a visit, he writes,

"I enjoyed seeing him at close range; I gazed upon him with astonishment, as upon a cask in which there had been millions and royal diamonds, reflecting on everything that had come forth from this man who sat beside me on a little chair and looking at his right hand that has written so many beautiful things. Here was the man who has made my heart beat most violently since I was born, and the one whom perhaps I loved most of all those I do not know."

Flaubert liked to say that one of the greatest emotions of his youth had been the reading of Goethe's *Faust.* He had read it in Rouen, on the Cours-la-Reine, that fine promenade planted with tall trees, on the left bank of the Seine. The church-bells, on the opposite bank, would resound in the air and mingle with Goethe's fine poetry.

"Christ is risen! Complete peace and joy . . . Do you already announce, deep bells, the first hour of Easter Day? Celestial canticle, strong and sweet, why do you seek me in the dust?"

His head would reel and he returned home as if dazed.

Beside such emotions, his first love impulses seem rather lacking in vividness. In the presence of a little English girl-friend of his sisters', who frightens him, he cannot overcome embarrassment. Then in Trouville, at the age of fifteen, he meets Marie Schlesinger, the wife of a big-business man; it is she, or rather the memory of this love, that he later transforms into Madame Arnoux, the heroine of *The Sentimental Education*. It seems that she was beautiful; she was thirteen years older than he; his feelings toward her were wholly platonic. But for Flaubert, who is imaginative and susceptible, the protective, maternal and inaccessible woman is the only kind he can love at that time. Soon this timidity is singularly heightened by illness. What was this nervous malady of Flaubert's? We do not know exactly. In any case it was such that it prevented him, during a great part of his life, from living in society. Whence his retirement to the little house in Croisset.

Yet he is known to have had one mistress, and what a mistress! Louise Colet . . . Louise Colet had almost all the great writers of this period for lovers. She was a superb woman, a poet who dedicated her pink complexion, her blond hair, and her lovely eyes to the service of her poetry. As the mistress of Victor Cousin, of Victor Hugo, of Alfred de Vigny, of Alfred de Musset, she received four times the Poetry Prize which those great men awarded. Maxime du Camp has said of her,

"She was pretty, rather stockily built, with an odd contrast between her features, which were delicate, and her demeanor, which was mannish. Heavy extremities, a harsh voice, betrayed an essential vulgarity."

But Maxime du Camp was not in love with her and was never quite fair to her.

Flaubert met her in 1846; he was twenty-five years old . . . Two months later she was his mistress. He seems to have loved her greatly. Yet she must quickly have irritated him. First by her literature, which was bad, and also by her letters and her conversation. If anyone in the world deserved to fill the *Dictionary of Accepted Ideas* with his remarks it was surely Louise Colet, for she uttered on the subject of love and of poetry all the imaginable platitudes. Toward the end of their relationship, Flaubert writes to her,

"I had expected to find in you a less feminine personality, a more universal conception of life . . . But no. The heart, the poor heart, that charming heart with

182

its eternal graces is always there, even among the highest . . ."

A gracious, courteous, tender manner, but a rather frank one, of confessing a disappointment. At the beginning he himself had rung the note of romantic love. His first letter is the letter of any young lover:

"Twelve hours ago, we were still together . . . How far away it already seems! The night now is warm and soft; I hear the tulip-tree, which is under my window, rustle in the wind and when I look up I see the moon reflected in the river. I am alone, and I have just arranged and put away safely all the things you gave me; your two letters are in the embroidered case; I shall re-read them when I have sealed mine . . . You are the only woman I have loved. One woman I loved from the age of fourteen to twenty without telling her, without touching her . . . I thought for a time that I would die so, and I thanked Heaven. You are the only one whom I have dared hope would like me, and perhaps the only one who has liked me. Thank you! Thank you! . . ."

Flaubert at a later time would have made fun of such phrases. However, he very quickly takes hold of himself. When Louise Colet sends him an orange blossom one can feel his exasperation,

"Thank you for your little orange blossom. Your whole letter is filled with its fragrance. Whether it was plucked from the tree, given by a man or a woman, it is no less beautiful to me, I assure you; it came from you, was sent by you, that is all I need. This attentiveness, by the way, touches me. I quite recognize you in this. How do you manage to get so much delight out of trifles, to give so much flavor to mere nothings?"

Then everything spoils:

"It seems to me that you are constantly taking me for something that I am not; now you make me out a kind of villain in a melodrama, and the next time you liken me to a traveling salesman. Between ourselves, I am neither so high nor so low. You vulgarize or poetize me too much. It's the old mania of women of ignoring the half-tones and not wanting to understand complex creatures—and there are so few simple souls! . . ."

"I have been so often humiliated, I have caused so many scandals, raised so many shouts, that I came to recognize a long time ago that in order to lead a quiet life one must live alone and seal all one's windows lest the air of society reach one. I always preserve in spite of myself something of this habit; this is why, for several years, I have systematically avoided the company of women."

Thibaudet believes that Flaubert loved Louise Colet to the point of deceiving himself as to the value of her work. Rereading the *Correspondence*, I have on the contrary the impression that there is at the beginning, in

Flaubert's eulogies, an element of amorous indulgence and an element of politeness; subsequently, an increasing dose of irritation.

In love as in friendship, he shows himself brutal, irascible, capable of violent revulsions. Louise Colet, after the break, would speak of "his monstrous personality, becoming increasingly exasperated in solitude" and also of "the being who, by his proud hardness, wielded an irresistible power over her." All this, no doubt, was true.

Louise Colet, through her artificial romanticism, unquestionably gave Flaubert certain of the elements out of which he was later to make *Madame Bovary*. He does not immediately utilize them. Before giving himself up to the fury of objectivity which will engender Madame Bovary, he feels the desire to express what, in his nature, "corresponded to Shakespeare and to Goethe". But when he had completed the *Temptation of Saint Anthony*, he read the manuscript to two of his most intimate friends, Maxime du Camp and Louis Bouilhet. They came to Croisset. The reading lasted more than thirty hours. When it was over, the two judges protested against the unbridled lyricism of the work. There was a long discussion in the garden in Croisset, a discussion which du Camp records for us:

" 'Since you have an irresistible tendency to lyricism,' said Maxime du Camp, 'you must choose a subject in which lyricism would be so ridiculous that you will be forced to guard yourself against it and give it up. Take a common-place subject, one of those incidents that bourgeois life is full of, and force yourself to treat it in a natural way.' "

Louis Bouilhet added,

" 'Why couldn't you write the story of Delamare?' "

Flaubert looked up, and joyfully exclaimed,

" 'What an idea! . . .' "

Delamare, a former student of Flaubert's father, had been a village doctor in Ry. He had taken for a second wife a girl named Delphine Couturier. Raised in a Rouen boarding-school, full of exaggerated ideas as to her own importance, she despised her husband; she ruined her household with her extravagance and improvidence; with her provocative airs, and her sensuality; she had lovers. Abandoned by these, pursued by creditors, she took poison. She left a daughter to whom Delamare became attached. But, in despair over the revelations each new day brought him as to his wife's conduct, he finally killed himself.

This is exactly the subject of *Madame Bovary*, a subject which satisfied the aesthetic needs of Flaubert, his desire to "expand small subjects," to "make a book out of nothing", his belief "that in literature there are no fine subjects, and that Yvetot is as good as Constantinople."

His lightning response, "What an idea!" to Bouilhet's suggestion proves, as Thibaudet believes, that his friend was preaching to one already converted.

When, in 1851, Flaubert harnesses himself to La Bovary, it may be said that his personal life (not his life as an artist but as a lover) is ended. In 1857 Jeanne de Loynes, the "Lady with the Violets", passes, very fleetingly, through his life. The rest is not worth describing. He begins *Madame Bovary* at the age of thirty, and Monsieur Maynial rightly says that "at this age he has already lived his whole life." From 1851 on, the story of his life is only the story of his work.

2. *MADAME BOVARY*

Charles Bovary, a country doctor and a widower, is called to attend a Norman big farmer, old Rouault, and here, by the sick-bed, meets the daughter, Emma. He is surprised by the whiteness of her nails, "shiny, delicate at the tips, more polished than the ivory of Dieppe and almond-shaped."

"Her real beauty was in her eyes. Although brown, they seemed black because of the lashes, and her look came at you frankly, with a candid boldness . . . Her neck stood out from a white turned-down collar. Her hair, whose two black folds seemed each of a single piece, so smooth were they, was parted in the middle by a delicate line that curved slightly with the curve of the head; and, just showing the tip of the ear, it was joined behind in a thick chignon, with a wavy line at the temples that the country doctor noticed now for the first time in his life. Like a man, she had a pair of tortoise-shell glasses slipped between the two buttons of her bodice."

He wishes to marry her; the father, too, is willing; Emma is bored in the country. Who knows? Perhaps this robust doctor would be the man of her dreams. One can tell how romantic she is by this little sentence, which occurs at the moment of the account of the wedding:

"Emma would have preferred to have a midnight wedding with torches; but old Rouault could not understand such an idea."

Charles Bovary is a disappointment to her:

"Before marriage she thought herself in love; but when the happiness that should have followed this love did not come she began to think she must have been mistaken. And Emma tried to imagine what, exactly, was meant by the words *felicity, passion* and *rapture,* that had seemed to her so beautiful in books."

In books . . . For it is an essential trait of Madame Bovary that she had formed her conception of life from books.

"She had read *Paul and Virginia* and she had dreamed of the little bamboo-house, the negro Domingo, the dog Fidèle, but above all of the sweet friendship of some dear little brother, who goes and picks red fruit for you in trees taller than steeples, or runs barefoot over the sand, bringing you a bird's nest."

The landscape of Normandy, where she lives, does not inspire her to lyricism; she knows it too well:

"She knew the lowing of cattle, the milking, the ploughs. Accustomed to calm aspects of life, she turned on the contrary to those of excitement. She loved the sea only for its storms, and green fields only when they appeared here and there among ruins. She had to get some kind of personal profit out of things; and she rejected as useless all that did not contribute to the immediate desires of her heart,—being of a temperament more sentimental than artistic, looking for emotions, not landscapes."

Only love-life, as it is depicted in novels, moves and tempts her:

"They were all love, lovers, sweethearts, persecuted ladies fainting in lonely pavilions, postilions killed at every stage, horses ridden to death on every page, sombre forests, heart-aches, vows, sobs, tears and kisses, little skiffs by moonlight, nightingales in shady groves, 'gentlemen' brave as lions, gentle as lambs, virtuous as no one

ever was, always well dressed, and weeping like foun-
tains."

At the convent everything had nourished her romanticism:

"In the music-class, in the ballads she sang, there was
nothing but little angels with golden wings, madonnas,
lagoons, gondoliers—mild compositions that allowed her
to glimpse, through the trivialities of style and the uncertainty of the notes, the attractive phantasmagoria of
emotional realities."

Romantic, too, were the engravings that she loved:

"Here behind the balustrade of a balcony was a young
man in a short cloak, holding in his arms a girl in a white
dress wearing an alms-bag at her belt; or anonymous portraits of English ladies with fair curls who looked at you
from under their round straw hats with their big bright
eyes . . . And you, too, were there, Sultans with long
pipes reclining beneath arbours in the arms of Bayaderes;
Djiaours, Turkish sabres, Greek caps; and you especially,
pale landscapes of dithyrambic lands, that often show us
at once palmtrees and firs, tigers on the right, a lion to the
left, Tartar minarets on the horizon, Roman ruins in the
foreground, and crouching camels;—the whole framed
by a well-groomed virgin forest, and with a great perpen-
dicular sunbeam trembling in the water, where, stand-

ing out in relief like white excoriations on a steel-gray ground, swans are swimming about."

Such were the elements of Emma Rouault's dreams before marriage.

When she met Charles, the only man she has been able to see intimately at her father's, because he is a doctor, the curiosity awakened by the presence of this stranger has made her believe that she was at last discovering the marvelous passion which she had divined in engravings, in music and in novels. Married, she cannot imagine to herself that the calm of her life with Charles is the happiness she has so often dreamed of.

Instead of living, she therefore continues to dream. She dreams of voyages, of abductions in post-chaises, behind blue silken curtains, of the sound of goat-bells and mountain cascades, of gulfs on whose shores one breathes the fragrance of lemon-trees. If Charles had been able to offer her travels, or at least to describe them, she would perhaps have been happy. But "Charles' conversation was commonplace as a street pavement, and every one's ideas trooped through it in their everyday garb . . . He could neither swim, nor fence, nor shoot . . . A man, she thought, should initiate a woman to the energies of passion, engage in manifold activities." Her husband is a disappointment to her.

The love that would satisfy Emma Bovary would be an

exotic, bookish love. Is this not, at bottom, love as Flaubert the adolescent once dreamed it? For Flaubert had to travel to the Orient and taste of Egyptian courtesans in order to convince himself of the vanity of his desires.

"Emma," Albert Thibaudet tells us, "incarnates the double illusion whose perception in Flaubert is still fresh. First the illusion in time . . . She does not believe things can appear the same at different times. And since the portion already lived had been bad, no doubt what remained to be consummated would be better. Then the same illusion in space . . . All that immediately surrounded her: the boring countryside, the imbecile petty bourgeois, the mediocrity of existence, seemed to her an exception in the world, a particular hazard in which she happened to be caught, while beyond, the immense country of expansive living and of passions spread out as far as the eye could reach."

This is romantic illusion in all its purity: the desire for escape in time and space.

So she repeats to herself, "Why, in Heaven's name, did I get married?" and wonders if there would not have been a way, by different combinations of destiny, to meet another man, for after all all men cannot be like this one. Does love exist? What can it be like? Unconsciously Emma looks about her, and first she meets the clerk Léon, a timid adolescent, who is a male replica of what she herself is as a woman. The conversations of Emma and Léon, both animated and ardent, almost painfully resemble conversations we have all known and carried on, alas! at the time of our first fumbling loves. Remarks that echo one another, a community of the commonplace, joy at discovering an identity of ideas which is but an identity of inanity:

"Have you taken any walks in the neighborhood?" Madame Bovary asks the young man.

He replies that he goes and watches the sunset.

" 'I think there is nothing so admirable as sunsets,' she resumed, 'but especially on the seashore . . .'

" 'Oh, I adore the sea!' said Léon.

" 'And then, does it not seem to you,' continued Madame Bovary, 'that the mind travels more freely on this limitless expanse, the contemplation of which elevates the soul and gives ideas of the infinite, the ideal?'

" 'It is the same with mountain landscapes,' Léon went on . . .''

"They felt the same languor stealing over them both . . . Overcome with wonder at this strange sweetness, they did not think of speaking of the sensation or of seeking its cause . . . They let themselves be lulled by this intoxication, without giving even a thought to the horizon that is beyond one's ken . . .''

Léon, in case of necessity, would be the desired lover. But he leaves Yonville without having dared.

The second hope is Rodolphe. He is the man of vigor, of brutal temperament, who has had many women and who judges them as a technician. He finds Madame Bovary pretty; the husband strikes him as stupid; he decides that he will make a conquest of the wife. He takes advantage of the Agricultural Show at Yonville to be alone with her in the midst of the crowd, and while the official personages distribute diplomas and medals to the live-stock raisers, to the old servants, Rodolphe murmurs in Emma's ear the ancient and banal phrases which have always assured certain men the conquest of women, as always the same maneuvers of envelopment by the wings have assured the winning of battles. Flaubert has taken cruel pleasure in alternating the imbecile speeches of the Fair with Rodolphe's platitudes. This central scene of the novel, an admirable literary exercise, is composed like a symphony in which two themes mingle and answer each other back and forth. There is something so mechanical in this alternation that at moments the tone seems rather that of comedy than that of the novel. But the effect of the sarcasm is powerful and these pages are perhaps those that best express the book's hard, melancholy lesson.

Naturally Madame Bovary lets herself rather easily be

won; but whereas Rodolphe is a simple and realistic fellow, Madame Bovary tries to lead him onto the literary plane. Into this bourgeois romance she would like to introduce scenes worthy of Walter Scott. When she makes a rendezvous with Rodolphe in her garden and he hears a noise, she says:

" 'Have you your pistols?'

" 'What for?'

" 'Why, to defend yourself!' replied Emma."

She keeps repeating to herself, "I have a lover . . . I have a lover. . . .," delighted at the idea:

"So at last she was to know those joys of love, that fever of happiness of which she had despaired. She was entering upon something marvelous where all would be passion, ecstasy, delirium; an azure infinity encompassed her, the heights of sentiment sparkled beneath her thought, and ordinary existence appeared only at a distance, far below in the shade, in the spaces between these heights . . . Then she recalled the heroines of the books that she had read and the lyric legion of those adulterous women began to sing in her memory with the voices of sisters that charmed her."

And as always happens the moment Emma falls in love, she dreams of traveling. She sees herself carried away with Rodolphe, to the gallop of four horses, toward a new country:

"Often from the top of a mountain they suddenly caught sight of some splendid city, with domes, bridges, ships, forests of lemon-trees, and cathedrals of white marble on whose pointed steeples storks had built their nests. They would go at a walking-pace because of the great flag-stones, and on the ground were bouquets of flowers which women dressed in red bodices would offer you . . . And then one night they came to a fishing village, where brown nets were drying in the wind along the cliffs and the row of huts. It was here that they would stop: they would live in a low, flat-roofed house, shaded by a palm-tree, in the heart of a gulf, by the sea. They would row in gondolas, swing in hammocks . . ."

She tries to make of Rodolphe the hero she has loved in Byron and he tries, up to a point, to lend himself to this. Having read a little himself, he would not be quite so incapable as Charles Bovary of playing the role that Emma assigns to him; but what he is unable to do is to endure the violence of passion for long. I should not be surprised if Flaubert, in depicting Rodolphe, had been inspired by his own attitude toward Louise Colet. Emma weepingly says:

" 'Oh! it is you I love! I love you so much that I cannot live without you, do you see? There are times when I long for you so much that I am torn by all the furies of love. I ask myself, 'Where is he? Perhaps he is talking to other women? They smile to him, he goes to them . . .' Oh, no, it isn't so, is it? None appeals to you? There are some prettier, but I can love better! I am your servant and your concubine! You are my king, my idol! You are good! You are handsome! You are intelligent! You are strong! . . ."

One can well imagine what would be Flaubert's answer to a letter from his mistress conceived in these terms.

Rodolphe's reaction is that he has already heard these things and that Emma is like all mistresses:

"The charm of novelty, gradually falling away like a garment, laid bare the eternal monotony of passion, which has always the same forms and the same language."

He does not understand that beneath Emma's words, which are indeed banal, there may yet be a true passion, and that human speech is "like a cracked pot on which we beat out melodies for bears to dance to, when we would like to move the stars." When Emma proposes to him to transform the dream into action and run away, he thinks only of separating from her.

"The worry, the expense! Ah! no, no! . . . It would have been too stupid . . ."

The break with Rodolphe marks the psychological center of the novel, as the scene of the Fair was its musical center, and it is the most serious crisis in Emma Bovary's life. Up to this point she has hoped that romantic love existed, and she has believed in it. The second part of the novel, as Faguet has clearly shown, is the slow disintegration of the first. This second part describes what little by little becomes of the romantic woman for whom romance has failed and who, while preserving her horror of reality, seeks to numb her suffering in pleasure, in the excitation of her senses. But between the two parts there is a period of transition. First Emma is ill, and illness is a wonderful form of escape. What is a madman, if not a romantic who thinks he is living his romance? Then she tries to save herself by coming back to her husband, by making herself love him. She would like to make a great man of him; perhaps, if she could feel esteem for him, she would learn to love him. From this stems the operation on the hotel-boy's club-foot which was to have made Charles Bovary famous, and which instead leads him to ruin and confusion. From this moment on, Emma drifts. To whom could she cling? Whom does she meet in this village? The pharmacist Homais? He is a solemn chatterer. The curate, Bournisien? He is a vulgar soul, without true faith.

At this moment, in the course of a trip to Rouen, she meets Léon, the young clerk who left Yonville without daring to confess his passion to her, and she becomes his mistress. But although she abandons herself to this ad-

198

venture with unreserved sensuality and heedlessness, she is again disappointed:

"They gradually came to talk more frequently of things unrelated to their love, and in the letters that Emma wrote him she spoke of flowers, verses, the moon and the stars, naive resources of a waning passion striving to keep itself alive by all external aids. She was constantly promising herself a deep felicity on her next journey. Then she had to admit to herself that she felt nothing extraordinary. This disappointment quickly gave way to a new hope, and Emma went back to him more inflamed, more avid than ever . . ."

Between reality and the dream the disproportion is greater than ever. She has wished for all the settings of poets, and her love-trysts take place in Rouen, in a hotel-room with Turkey-red curtains. She falls into the hands of the dealer Lheureux, who makes her sign notes and who ruins her. Flaubert, in his plan, described this period thus:

"She becomes sensual. She enjoys everything: perfume, flowers, food, wines . . . She spends hours at her toilet, and sitting before her dressing table in sandals she experiences a voluptuous thrill as she combs her hair that falls over her shoulders. She no longer wears anything but cambric. The despair of unassuaged comfort comes to the support of the atavistic need for luxury . . . The impulse to lie develops in her. She gets hold of the money of the clients and the tradespeople. She has spent Léon. She does not love him for himself, but for her own sake, and rather despises him. He is a coward. He is afraid of compromising himself . . . Lack of money . . . Progress of the financial ruin . . . Bills rain down on her . . . Perplexity . . . Last expedients . . . She is humiliated at having loved Léon so much and comes to realize the femininity of this pathetic creature . . ."

In the disorders of her affairs, it occurs to her to turn to Rodolphe. He harshly dismisses her. She goes to see an old notary, who perhaps would help her *if* . . . But *la Romanesque* is not for sale. She then enters the shop of Homais the pharmacist, steals some arsenic and poisons herself. She dies a horrible death, "a disproportionate penalty," it has been said, "for her crimes which after all were not so serious." But Flaubert is not a judge, and it is not love that kills Madame Bovary: she dies because she has refused life, because she has wanted to live a dream.

3. *BOVARYSM*

This world that Flaubert creates is indeed gloomy. In Yonville-l'Abbaye, there is not a single being with whom one would wish to spend a few hours a day, let alone strike up a friendship. Emma is undoubtedly wrong in asking of life what is to be found only in romantic novels. But it must be confessed that the cards are stacked against her. If life cannot offer every loving woman her hero, at least it gives to many women a man it is possible to love. Emma Bovary does not meet a single one. Charles Bovary? There is no harm in him, but neither is there intelligence nor anything to command respect. He is an incarnation of that "bourgeois" vulgarity which Flaubert hated. But he could have been a mediocre husband, a poor lover, and still been a competent doctor. Yet he fails no less spectacularly in his profession than in his household. Charles Bovary is neither a remarkable practitioner, nor an agreeable life companion, nor a sexual partner. He is nothing. He is unfortunate.

And Madame Bovary's lovers are no better than her husband. Rodolphe? A professional lady-killer, who considers the woman as an instrument. He is selfish, cowardly, and on no consideration does he want the risks of an adventure. He is even close-fisted, and when Emma in despair asks him for eight thousand francs, he claims that he does not have the sum, which is highly improbable. Léon? He lacks courage to win Emma in the course of their first encounter, and courage to keep her in the course of the second. He also is a coward.

Again, fate treats Emma Bovary more badly than it treats most Frenchwomen. With a little luck it should have been possible to find a man, in Yonville or in Rouen, who would be happy to dedicate himself to this young woman, who was a little exacting, to be sure, but pretty and agreeably romantic.

Emile Faguet maintained that Emma could have been very happy if she had married Homais. This is not impossible, for she was not sufficiently intelligent to judge Homais' erudition and vocabulary severely. She would no doubt have been proud of her husband's eloquence, which she would quickly have imitated. Besides, there was solid stuff in Homais. Well backed by a clever woman, he would have succeeded. When Emma received at her table Doctor Larivière and the editor-in-chief of the *Fanal de Rouen*, she would have charmed them both. To please her, they would have decided the fate of the pharmacist's writings. Eulogistic accounts of them would have been published. In Flaubert's book, Homais obtains the Croix d'Honneur in the end. Who knows how far he might have gone, with Emma? Even without her, Thibaudet can easily imagine him a General Councilor, and a Senator from the Seine-Inférieure, and this is quite plausible. And finally she would have had many children, for Homais is a formidable procreator. There is nothing better for curing a romantic woman! She would not even have deceived him.

But an endurable Charles Bovary, a passionate and faithful Rodolphe, a virile Léon, would not have suited Flaubert's purposes. Flaubert did not want Emma to be saved, because he did not believe humanity could be saved. "*I* am Madame Bovary," he would say . . . Now in his own case, romanticism had failed on the plane of reality as on the plane of art. He had had to curb his lyricism like his sentiments and, if we try to reconstruct the stages of his thought, this is approximately what we find:

a) Romanticism is inevitable. Every being tries to escape from himself. He may run away in space, and this is exoticism (Flaubert's study was littered with exotic objects), or in time, and then he writes *Salammbô*, the *Temptation of Saint Anthony* if he is Flaubert; he reads Walter Scott or Dumas the elder if he is not himself a creator of myths. Flaubert (and his characters like himself) dream life and do not live it. "Every notary carries within himself the debris of a poet." All try "to imagine themselves different from what they are." This is what Jules de Gaultier has very fittingly called *le Bovarysme*.

b) But romanticism always fails, because it pursues the inaccessible. Always the dreamer's destiny goes awry because always external circumstances are hostile to the dream. The true subject of *Madame Bovary* is the increasingly great gap between circumstances and the dream. Emma desires to love Tristan or Lancelot; she meets Rodolphe and Léon; she ends in the clutches of the merchant Lheureux, who is reality's revenge in its most sordid form.

In Flaubert's view guilt attached, not to what Emma and Léon desire, but to desire itself. The wise man must want nothing. The best that we possess is the happiness we have refused to pluck. Every dream resembles the Zaïmph, the sacred veil of *Salammbô*. Whoever touches it dies of the contact.

One must therefore despise the temptations of the world. Saint Anthony is punished for having yielded to them. But also Frederick, in *The Sentimental Education* . . . Frederick becomes a bourgeois because he accepts a commonplace happiness. Emma Bovary ends by being condemned to suicide, because she has attempted to transpose into daily existence what should have remained in the realm of dream. At the beginning of her marriage, when she is still the pure Romantic Woman, she holds off the foul Lheureux. At the end of her life she capitulates; she wants to possess *in reality* scarves, riding crops, and all the accessories of her rôle as a romantic woman. It is by this that she is ruined.

Where would salvation lie? Flaubert, like Proust, sees salvation only for the artist. Since the world is illusion, one can merely describe it. The only universe is that which the artist creates. Man cannot imagine what he possesses. It is not lyrical subjectivity that will make great novelists or great poets. "You will paint wine, love, glory, on condition, my good fellow, that you become neither a drunkard, a lover, nor a soldier-boy." And elsewhere he says, "If I had been loved at seventeen, what a cretin I should be now!"

In other words, one must choose between life and art. Autobiography itself is never true. The true autobiography is that which the novelist writes *without knowing it,* behind the screen of a fiction which appears objective to him. This is the profound meaning of the famous remark, "*I* am Madame Bovary . . ."

4. EMMA BOVARY AND OUR TIME

Does Madame Bovary remain a universal type? She probably does. I have met her even in America. There, Charles Bovary is a bank teller, a grocery clerk, an assistant professor, when Emma Rouault Bovary would want him to be President of the United States, a partner in the Morgan Bank, or a male star in Hollywood. This American Bovary seeks refuge in the fictions of the screen rather than in those of novels; she expects from life what the big films reveal of it; she is disappointed because most men, in America as elsewhere, are average beings.

Average, but not devoid of interest. Herein lies the immense, the fearful error of all the Bovarys. They are so ardent in their pursuit of romantic love that they no longer see human love, which would bring them happiness. If Emma had taken the trouble to observe Charles Bovary, if she had been content to share with him the simple joys which were within his scope, and to find in her readings other joys which she could have reserved for herself, she might have led in Yonville a quite tolerable existence. But because she committed the error of confusing the plane of art with that of life, she detested Yonville. To which it may be answered that it is not well to find Yonville tolerable, that one must surpass Yonville, and that civilizations are improved only by those who hate them.

Endless discussions, these, which Flaubert would have condemned. A novel, he would have repeated again, is not a lesson in morality.

"What seems to me the highest in art, and the most difficult, is neither to make men laugh, nor to make them weep, but to do as nature does, namely to make them dream. And this is the character of the very finest works.

They are serene in aspect, and incomprehensible in their processes; they are motionless as cliffs, tumultuous as the sea, full of foliage, greennesses and murmurs like the woods, melancholy as the desert, blue as the sky. Homer, Rabelais, Michelangelo, Shakespeare, Goethe strike me as pitiless. Their work is bottomless, infinite, multiple. Through little apertures one perceives precipices; there is blackness at the bottom, dizziness, and yet something singularly troubling hovers over the whole. It is the ideal of light, the smile of the sun, and it is calm; it is calm and it is strong . . ."

Such is Madame Bovary. Was she a sinner, a fool, or a heroine? No matter! She exists. We know her. She appears to us with her little turned-down white collar, the day Charles Bovary, on the farm, sees her for the first time. She slips off her clothes with a single movement, in the room with the Turkey-red curtains in the Hôtel des Empereurs at Rouen. She slowly passes her hand through Charles's hair, as she lies dying. As Flaubert would have it, she awakens, not judgment, but revery. The philosopher Hegel, in the presence of mountains, found only this to say: "That's how it is." Before the very great works of art, this is also the only remark that comes to our lips. Because a very great artist has depicted it, we can contemplate that little Norman town and find it "bottomless, infinite, multiple". Like the great religious mystics, Flaubert, a mystic of art, found his recompense in a vision that transcends time. And as the believer, because he humiliates himself, shall be saved, the romantic Flaubert, because one day he accepted the humblest of subjects, wrote the most illustrious, and the most rightly illustrious of French novels.

SEVEN

LOVE, REALITY OR ILLUSION?

Heroines of Marcel Proust

HE CONDEMNATION of the romantic by Flaubert could not be accepted by women as a permanent solution to emotional problems. And the women were right, and Flaubert wrong. For by dint of imagining more beautiful forms of love, one ends by creating them; this had been clearly shown in the time of chivalry. The whole problem is to deal patiently with transitions and slowly to bring together the reality and the dream. To this the novelists who followed Flaubert dedicated themselves.

After Zola's naturalism, which was a romanticism of

science, Guy de Maupassant, Paul Bourget, Anatole France painted voluptuous pictures of adultery in high society, veiled by eloquent or witty language, which may well have perverted more than one Parisian Emma Bovary. But none of them achieved the depth of the analyses of Stendhal and all three are minor novelists, Maupassant (particularly in *One Life*) being of the three the most human.

Toward the end of the nineteenth century a philosophy appeared—that of Bergson—which advised artists to go beyond words and re-discover, beneath those impersonal labels, the living passions which a hardened, congealed, language conceals. Even as certain painters at the same time were endeavoring, through a conventional nature, to reach true Nature, so a novelist, Marcel Proust, was to show that if the writer refuses to accept the classic picture of the passions of love, he may discover a poetic reality lying beyond the traditional vocabulary.

1. PROUST'S PLACE

Marcel Proust's characters, like those of Madame de La Fayette, are creatures of leisure. Like her, he paints a society of idlers who have enough time and discrimination to analyze their feelings. It might be said that the characters of *In Search of the Past* (*Remembrance of Things Past*) are direct descendants of those of *The Princess of Clèves*. They belong to the same world; they live in the same drawing rooms, and Monsieur de Nemours was surely, in the seventeenth century, a cousin of the Guermantes. But if the setting and the characters are the same, the attitude of the author toward his heroes and his manner of describing their feelings have greatly changed.

For Madame de La Fayette and for Jean-Jacques Rousseau, *love has an absolute value*. Rousseau never asks himself whether Saint-Preux really loves Julia, how this love was born, whether Saint-Preux might not just as easily love any other woman. Madame de La Fayette herself does not imagine for a moment that the Princess of Clèves loves Monsieur de Nemours by mere chance; she is careful to indicate that he is the most "worthy to be loved" of the gentlemen of the court. The Princess of Clèves and Julia are loved because, in the eyes of their creators, they wholly deserve to be loved: beautiful, intelligent, perfect, true novel-heroines.

Stendhal, already more sceptical, begins to break down the mechanism of passion. He studies crystallization; he knows that, if circumstances had been different, Julien would not have loved Mathilde, nor Fabrice Clelia. At least his intelligence knows it, but if Stendhal's mind is that of a *libertin*, we have shown that *his heart remains as susceptible* as Jean-Jacques'. Although he understands crystallization, he crystallizes. He even crystallizes on his own heroines. He is quite literally in love himself with Madame de Rênal and Clelia Conti. He depicts women infinitely more perfect than the real women he has been able to observe. The word *heroine* still quite properly designates them.

As for Flaubert, he no longer believes in romantic love. He is the Homais of the religion of love, the Voltairian of romanticism. An Homais who is a great artist. But just as the pharmacist of Yonville failed to understand the reality of religion and the efficacy of its help, so Flaubert forgets the real power of love. The heroes of novels had perhaps been too romantic; Rodolphe and Léon are not romantic enough; I mean that they are even less so than most real men. Emma is no longer a "heroine"; *she dreams that she is a heroine*, which is quite different.

Finally Proust, who is the subject of the present study, believes in the reality of love, in the strength of the feelings which it inspires, in the violence of the sufferings which it inflicts, *but he no longer believes*, like Madame de La Fayette or Rousseau, *that the violence of these passions is made legitimate by the exceptional quality of the beings who are its objects*. We shall see that he considers passionate love as a malady—inevitable, painful and fortuitous. Little does it matter in his view what the specific value of the loved one may be. Just as a tiny germ can bring us down with a high fever, so the most insignificant woman can make us very unhappy. We shall have to show that the peculiar character of the heroines of Proust is that they exist only in the mind of him who loves them.

To sum up, Madame de La Fayette had studied love as a metaphysician, Rousseau as a moralist, Laclos as a cynic, Stendhal as a lover, Balzac as a collector, Flaubert as an unbeliever and an iconoclast. Proust studies it both as a poet and a clinician.

With unequalled intelligence and precision, Proust has several times described the evolution, the symptoms and the cure of this malady of love. It is, in a sense, the subject of his whole novel and particularly of the story of Albertine; but in the first of the seven volumes he expounds its themes succinctly, and in an admirable way, in what could be a self-contained little novel which is set like a jewel in the larger work of *In Search of the Past*, and whose title is *Swann in Love*. It is here that we must first study the course of the disease, which according to Proust is always identical.

2. *SWANN IN LOVE*

Now Swann, who is a friend of Marcel's parents, a very cultivated, very refined Jew, who spends most of his time in the aristocratic society of the Guermantes and could have as mistresses the most remarkable women in this circle, one day by chance, in a theatre, meets a woman, Odette de Crécy, to whom a friend of his introduces him. She appears to Swann, not without beauty, but having a kind of beauty which is indifferent to him, which stimulates in him no desire, and which even arouses in him a kind of physical repulsion. Every man has "his type", probably born of mysterious early impressions (Schopenhauer claimed that this type is for each one of us complementary to our own, but this is more complex). Now, Odette does not appeal to Swann because her profile is too sharp, her skin too fragile, her cheek-bones too prominent. Her eyes are beautiful, but too big. Besides, what he knows about her does not predispose him to her. She has the reputation of being fast, perhaps even mercenary. She lacks refinement, sometimes to the point of vulgarity. In short, she not only is not Swann's "type", but she is exactly the opposite.

Some days after this meeting, Odette writes to Swann to ask his permission to see his collections. She comes to his house, and each time he sees her he is sad at the thought that this great beauty is not of the kind that he likes. But each time she leaves him, he smiles on remembering her telling him that time would hang heavily on her hands until the next time he would allow her to come back. He remembers the anxious, timid air with which she begged him "not to let it be too long," and a look of timorous imploring which at that moment made her appealing.

In these first meetings, Odette makes great efforts to attract Swann and to introduce him to the little clan in which she lives, which is the salon of Madame Verdurin. Meanwhile, without being aware of it, Swann is beginning vaguely to "crystallize" in relation to Odette. He is touched by her attentions, and one day when he visits her, Swann (who is an art lover and who has always enjoyed trying to discover the features of faces he knows in the paintings of the masters) is suddenly struck by Odette's resemblance to the figure of Zephora, the daughter of Jethro, that appears in a fresco of Botticelli's in the Sistine Chapel. From this moment the resemblance confers on Odette a beauty which makes her more precious. We have seen in Stendhal how the crystallization may be brought about in each love by circumstances which are different, but always linked to a dominant passion. If I am a great sportsman, I shall be touched by the skill a woman shows in getting on a horse, in playing golf. An Englishman will "crystallize" on a tennis champion; a musician on a singer; a statesman on a woman who shares his political passions. Swann, a lover of painting, crystallizes on a pictorial beauty. He reproaches himself for having misjudged the charm of a creature whom Botticelli would have worshipped and he says to himself that this inclination which she seems to show for him is not, after all, something indifferent (even though her face appears imperfect to him), but something rare, since Odette satisfies in him his most refined love of art:

"The expression *Florentine work* rendered Swann a great service. Like a title, it enabled him to introduce Odette's image into a world of dreams to which she had not had access until now and which infused her with nobility. And while the purely fleshly view he had had of this woman, perpetually renewing his doubts as to the quality of her face, of her body, of her whole beauty, weakened his love, these doubts were destroyed, this love assured, when instead it had the data of an infallible aesthetic for a base; without counting the fact that kisses and possession, which seemed natural and mediocre if they were accorded him by a bit of worn flesh must, he thought, be supernatural and delightful when on the contrary they became the crowning ritual in the worship of a museum-piece."

The crystallization being now assured by the aesthetic link, Swann goes every night to Madame de Crécy's, and as he is now in love he finds charm only in things to which Odette confers it. But the crystallization, in Swann who is a voluptuous egotist, would undoubtedly not be very deep were it not abetted by the element which Stendhal has already described to us as the most important, which is doubt. Swann, who sees Odette only at night and who knows nothing as to the way in which she spends her time during the whole day, begins to perceive that there is a portion of Odette's life that is unknown to him. To escape doubt he tries to draw closer to Odette, and since the only way to see her constantly is to become a part of the same group as she, Swann, ordinarily so discriminating in the choice of his relations, becomes a humble frequenter of the rather vulgar "little circle" that meets at the Verdurins. And, as happens to all men the moment they fall in love, he comes to enjoy the society of the Verdurins because when he is with them he can enjoy the sight of Odette, her presence, her conversation. His intelligence and his critical sense cease to function.

" 'What a charming group!' he said to himself. 'That, after all, is really the only way to live! How much more intelligent, more artistic, they are than society. And in spite of her little exaggerations that are rather laughable, how sincere Madame Verdurin's love of painting and

SEVEN FACES OF LOVE

music is! What a passion for works of art! What a desire to give pleasure to artists! . . . And above all, you
feel free there, you can do what you want without re-
straint, without ceremony . . . But for some rare ex-
ceptions, I shall certainly never become a part of any
other group . . .' "

The virtues that the lover thinks he discovers in the
Verdurins are but the reflection upon them of the
pleasures that flatter his passion for Odette. Proust derives infinite enjoyment from portraying the stupidity of
the intimates of the Verdurin salon because the more
manifest their absurdities are the more remarkable will
be the paralysis of Swann's intelligence, led astray by
love. We recognize the first symptoms of the malady.
The rule might be more generally stated thus: as soon as
a man begins to go around saying that a woman, of average or even mediocre capacities, is "admirably intelligent", or "very artistic", it is because he is feeling the first
effects of the disease.

Odette, who is now sure of Swann, has for her part
ceased to crystallize. And little by little Swann discovers
that outside of him she leads a whole mysterious life in
the course of which she undoubtedly deceives him.
Doubt becomes jealousy, in other words, a deep curiosity
for the slightest actions of the loved being. Love, in

Proust's view, is not so much desire for physical possession as desire for emotional and intellectual possession.
The lover seeks to identify with the soul of the other; he
would like to see it whole and bright spread out before
him. Until then a woman's daily acts and gestures had
always appeared negligible to Swann. He had considered the gossip of women about other women trivial
and commonplace; but in the strange period of love
which is jealousy, "the particular takes on something so
profound that this awakening curiosity that Swann felt
in regard to Odette's slightest occupations was the very
same that he had once had for History."

It is not long before he discovers that Odette is a liar.

" 'Even from the simple point of view of coquetry,' he
said to her, 'don't you realize how much of your seductive-
ness you lose by stooping to lying? Really, you are much
less intelligent than I thought.' "

But Odette, like all creatures who are instinctive
mythomaniacs, cannot help distorting the truth. Besides, by her lies and by the atmosphere of curiosity into
which these plunge Swann, Odette keeps her hold over
him much more surely than if she had a frank and noble
soul. (I do not think this observation would be true of
all men, but it is true of Swann, who has a great deal of
leisure and time to meditate endlessly on Odette's
secrets.)

Finally Swann reaches the point of suffering excruciating torments, all because of this extremely commonplace woman. He knows that "the others" could only consider his love as childishness and madness. But for him this love is everything. Listening one day, during a concert, to the playing of the violin it seems to him that a certain little musical phrase alone sees in his love what he himself finds there: something so greatly superior to actual life that he is ready to sacrifice this life to his love. Little by little the relation grows closer. Swann obtains proof that Odette is unfaithful to him, and yet he ties himself irremediably to Odette. But later, having become lucid again, he will say to himself,

"And to think that I have wasted several years of my life, that I have wanted to die, that I have had my greatest love, for a woman who did not appeal to me, who was not my kind!"

An admirable, and essential sentence, a sentence that contains one of the most important elements of Proust's doctrine on love: *"I have wanted to die for a woman who was not my kind . . ."* For the disease that is love brings into conflict our conscious intelligence and our basic will. In rare moments of lucidity, we can indeed still see this man (or this woman) objectively, as normal beings—others—can, but subjectively imprisoned in our inner world, we have ceased to see them. We know nothing more of them than the feeling with which they inspire us. Are they beautiful? Are they ugly? Intelligent or stupid? Genuine or contemptible? We no longer even know. We need them. Therein lie both our disease and the greatness of our attachment.

Such is the first sketch, by Marcel Proust, of the cycle of love. All its themes are taken up again in a new way in *Within a Budding Grove* (*A l'Ombre des Jeunes Filles en Fleurs*). The hero, a sickly young man, taken to the seashore, to Balbec, by his grandmother, sees a group of young girls pass on the beach. He knows nothing about them, but he notices in passing a girl with bright, laughing eyes, with big moist cheeks, wearing a black polo jumper, who pushes a bicycle with such an ungainly swinging of her hips and using such vulgar *argot* terms, shouting so loudly, that he has the impression these young persons are the mistresses of bicycle racers. At the moment when he comes abreast of this big-cheeked brunette he catches her laughing, sidelong glance. Does she see him? And if she sees him, what can he represent for her? Obviously nothing.

The pathos of this encounter strikes us particularly when we re-read the novel after having finished it, because we know that this girl, Albertine, is going to become the center of the hero's life, that he will come to be so jealous of the least minutes of Albertine's time that he will shut her up and watch her like a prisoner, and that long after Albertine's death he will continue to suffer for and through her. And yet at the first moment she had been no more to him than what she really was: a blooming, big-cheeked girl who spoke too loudly. As she passes, he hears her utter an expression he detests, "Living your life . . ." She is not his kind, any more than Odette was Swann's kind, but circumstances enter into play, and little by little a fictive creature takes the place of the real Albertine.

The crystallization, in the case of *Within a Budding Grove*, occurs because Marcel, constantly seeing that little group on the beach, makes a game of trying to anticipate their movements. As their habits are unknown to him and he notices that there are days when they do not appear, he tries in spite of himself to discover why. Is this absence regular? Does it occur every two days? Or every three days? Does it correspond to some use of their time? Or to atmospheric circumstances? The observation of the irregular movements of this unknown world creates in the mind that curiosity so favorable to the birth of love.

"To the first uncertainty as to whether I would see them or not was added another, more serious one: whether I should never see them again. For after all I did not know whether they might not be leaving for

America, or returning to Paris. This was enough to make me begin to love them. One may have an inclination for a person; but in order to be overcome by that melancholy, that feeling of the irreparable, those anguishes that prepare love, one must have the feeling of an impossibility."

Little by little, as he gets to know Albertine better, the real being takes shape by a process of trial and error. He comes to realize that the girl he has so much desired to know, the stranger on the beach, has no connection with the one he has at last managed to be introduced to:

"From that first day I realized what a hocus-pocus had been perfectly executed and how thanks to the skill of the magician, I had chatted for a moment with a person who, without having any resemblance to the one I had watched for so long on the seashore, had been substituted for her. I might, for that matter, have guessed it beforehand, since the girl on the beach had been manufactured by me. In spite of this, I felt a moral obligation to her to keep the promises of love made to an imaginary Albertine. One becomes betrothed by proxy, and one subsequently considers oneself obliged to marry the interposed person."

In other words, around a face, a figure that we have glimpsed, we construct an imaginary being; with this being, in a sense secreted by ourselves, we fall in love; then when, later on, we discover the quite different real being who is attached to that face, we accept him and transfer to him the feelings born of a fiction.

Finally, a third example of this subjectivity of love: the case of Rachel and Saint-Loup. Robert de Saint-Loup, a young man of noble character as well as rank, talks constantly to Marcel about a mistress whom he considers the rarest being he has met. Now when he introduces her to his friend, the latter recognizes with stupefaction a woman who gives herself, for a little money, to anyone who wants her and to whom, for this reason, he has never attached any importance.

"I realized all that a human imagination can put behind a little bit of a face, as this woman's was, if it is imagination that has first known her; and, inversely, into what wretched material elements, shorn of all value, without price, could be decomposed what was the object of so many reveries if, on the contrary, one had come to know it in a different way, by the most trivial kind of acquaintance . . . To be sure, it was the same thin and narrow face that Robert and I saw, but we had reached it by two opposite roads that would never meet, and we should never see the same aspect of it. This face, with its glances, its smiles, the movements of its mouth, I had known from the outside as being attached to some nondescript body which for twenty francs would do anything I asked. And so the glances, the smiles, the movements of the mouth had appeared to me only as signifying certain general acts, without anything individual about them, and beneath them I should not have been curious to look for a person. But what had in a sense been offered to me at the start—this consenting face—had been for Robert a destination toward which he had traveled through how many hopes, doubts, suspicions, dreams. He was paying more than a million to possess—so that it should not be offered to others—what had been offered to me, as to anyone else, for twenty francs . . . Looking at her, the two of us, we did not see her from the same side of the mystery . . ."

Once again, in the case of Rachel, Proust has shown us that love depends, not on the quality of the loved being, but on the emotions of the being who loves and on the circumstances which, in the mind of the latter, have deformed the objective images. And just as Marcel cannot understand Robert de Saint-Loup's love for Rachel, Robert in turn, seeing only the real Albertine, cannot understand the violence of Marcel's feelings.

"What had put Robert out of countenance when he had perceived Albertine's photograph was not the thrill of the Trojan old men seeing Helen pass and saying, 'Our misfortune is not worth a single one of her glances,' but exactly the opposite shock, which makes a person say,

"'What? It is for this that he has worried, suffered, committed so many follies!'"

A false reasoning; no one commits follies for Helen, but for the image of Helen, for the myth of Helen. Let us leave pretty women, Proust concludes, to men without imagination; men who have imagination will see Helen in any woman.

3. *THE ILLUSIONS OF LOVE*

From these examples we must now try to elucidate Proust's doctrine on love. The goal he seems to be setting himself is to destroy the ready-made ideas that most human beings form on this subject, and that literature helps to spread. What are these ready-made ideas? We have seen, in the novels we have studied, how the traditional novelists had been accustomed to describe the course of love. A description which, moreover, complied with the desires of readers. Men and women like to believe in "love at first sight", in some mysterious predestination which supposedly brings together a given man and a given woman (or, for that matter, a given man and a given man, a given woman and a given woman), in a perfect union of body and spirit. The secret wish of all lovers is that this attachment, born of the moment, should be eternal. Their vows affirm this eternity; forgetfulness, at the time of the "first sight", seems an improbable and even blameworthy hypothesis.

Does this picture of love correspond to reality, as a lucid novelist observes it? Proust answers, "No." Love, he tells us, is not a bond between us and a given loved person; it is a need which is in ourselves at certain moments of our existence, and in particular at the time of adolescence. We begin by being in love, which is a state, like being hungry. Then we say to ourselves, "Whom am I in love with?" Then the actresses, young or old, appear, wishing to be given the rôle. How shall we choose between them? Often it is a matter of chance. It may happen that we have met Albertine or Andrée on the beach, that Rachel has been introduced to us by a procuress, that the Duchesse de Guermantes lives in the mansion at the end of our courtyard. Many men, if they were to ask themselves why the woman who has filled their lives interested them in the beginning, and if they were able sincerely to analyze the situation, would be stupefied by the childishness, the pettiness of their reasons for the choice. If on that morning, we had gone into the next compartment; if we had refused that luncheon, our whole love-life would have been different.

227

"The woman whose face we have before us more constantly than light itself—since, even with our eyes shut, we do not cease for a moment to cherish her lovely eyes, her lovely nose, to do everything we can to see them again—this unique woman, we know, could very well have been replaced by another woman if we had been in another town than the one where we met her, if we had been walking in another district, if we had been moving in a different circle. Unique, we think—and she is innumerable. Yet she is compact, indestructible before our eyes that love her, irreplaceable for a very long time by another. It is because this woman has merely stirred up, by a kind of magic spell, a thousand elements of tenderness existing in ourselves in a fragmentary state and which she has gathered together, united, effacing every break between them; it is ourselves who, by endowing her with her features, have furnished all the solid substance of the loved person."

More than this, it is *because* we know so little about this loved person that we attach ourselves to her with so much force. Odette appears to Swann as a vulgar, uncultivated woman, who is in short quite uninteresting as long as he thinks he knows everything about her. It is from the moment when she contains a mystery that she begins to touch him. The Girls in the Bloom of Youth intrigue Marcel and hold him because they are living mysteries for him. On certain days he meets them on the beach of Balbec, but on other days they do not appear. Why? What are the laws of their apparitions? Are their movements, to ever so slight an extent, commanded by his? Are they avoiding him or seeking him out? From the moment when we ask ourselves such questions, we "crystallize" and we feel the first effects of the malady which is love. "The charms of a person," Proust writes, "are as frequent a cause of love as a remark like this, 'No, tonight I'm not free . . .'" Alain, the philosopher, used to say, "Women derive their glamour from being late and from being absent." Why? Because absence and lateness create mystery, anxiety, and "that anxious need" which is one of the symptoms of the disease.

The pre-existing and mobile love "stops at the image of a certain woman because this woman will be almost impossible to win."

"From then on one thinks less of the woman, whom it is difficult to visualize, than of the means of knowing her. A whole process of anguish develops and suffices to attach our love to her, who, barely known to us, becomes its object. Love becomes immense; we no longer reflect upon how small a place the real woman occupies in it . . . What did I know of Albertine? One or two glimpses of her profile against the sea . . ."

229

But Albertine is a liar, and even a mythomaniac, and hereby she is immediately endowed with that odious glamour of mystery. Because he does not understand her, Marcel wishes to keep her under his surveillance, possess her both in the general and in the special sense of the word. He vainly hopes to free himself thus, but this is another illusion. Physical possession, in Proust's eyes, is but a quasi-negligible element in the poison of love. Men believe that those sensations, so much vaunted, are the essential object of their desires, but they seek them only as proof of a more complete possession which, however, is unattainable. This is so true that in themselves the physical sensations of love are frankly disagreeable. Witness how Proust describes the moment when, after so many days of expectation and hope, he is at last able to kiss Albertine:

"Before kissing her I should very much have liked to be able again to endow her with the mystery that she had for me on the beach, before I knew her, to find in her again the country where she had previously lived; instead, since I did not know her, I could at least slip in all the memories of our life in Balbec, the sound of the wave breaking under my window, the children's cries. But, as I let my eyes glide over the lovely pink swelling of her cheeks, whose softly curved-in surfaces came washing up against the feet of the first folds of her beautiful black hair that ran in undulating chains, lifted their abrupt spurs and shaped the deep course of their valleys, I had to say to myself,

" 'At last, since I was unable to do so in Balbec, I am going to know the taste of the unknown roses that are the cheeks of Albertine . . .'

"I said this to myself because I believed that there is a kind of knowledge to be obtained by the lips. I said to myself that I was going to know the taste of this fleshly rose because I had not considered that man, a creature obviously less rudimentary than the sea-urchin or even the whale, nevertheless still lacks a certain number of essential organs, and notably possesses none that is adequate for a kiss. This missing organ he supplies with his lips, and thereby he perhaps achieves a somewhat more satisfying result than if he were reduced to caressing his beloved with horned tusks. But the lips, made to bring to the palate the flavor of something that tempts them, unable to understand that error and to admit their disappointment, must content themselves with roaming over the surface and beating against the wall of the impenetrable and desired cheek. Moreover, at that moment, at the very contact of the flesh, even assuming that they became more expert and better endowed, the lips would no doubt be unable to taste more fully the flavor that nature actually prevents their seizing, for in this desolate zone where they cannot find their nourishment they are alone, having long since been abandoned by sight, and then by smell. First, as my mouth gradually began to approach cheeks that my eyes had suggested to them that they kiss, the latter as they moved saw new cheeks: the neck perceived at closer range and as if through a magnifying glass, showed in its rougher texture a robustness that modified the character of the face . . . Just as in Balbec Albertine had often appeared different to me, so now, in the short journey of my lips toward her cheeks, I saw ten Albertines; this single girl being like a goddess with several heads, the one I had seen last, if I tried to approach it, gave way to another. At least so long as I had not touched it I could see this head, and its faint fragrance reached me. But alas!—for our nostrils and our eyes are as inadequately placed for kissing as our lips are badly made—suddenly my eyes ceased to see; my nose, in turn, becoming crushed, no longer perceived any smell, and without knowing the desired rose-taste any better I learned, by those detestable signs, that at last I was kissing Albertine's cheek."

If this is true of a kiss, so it is with complete carnal possession. Neither can make us master of her whom we love.

4. *THE CAPTIVE AND THE DEAD*

But if what men are accustomed to call "the pleasures of love" does not create passionate love, what does create it? According to Proust, as we have seen, it is *suffering*, and in particular that suffering which is born of doubt. Certainty (this was already an idea of Stendhal's) robs love of all charm:

"Imagination, awakened by the uncertainty of being able to attain its object, must create a goal which conceals from us the other, and by substituting for sensual pleasure the idea of entering into a life, prevent us from recognizing this pleasure, from perceiving its true taste, from confining it within its own scope, for to strip our pleasures of imagination is to reduce them to themselves, to nothingness."

Of these uncertainties, the most painful—and consequently the one which, if we are to believe Proust, brings beings closest to each other—is jealousy. It may sometimes become so horrible that in order to calm our anguish we come to wish the loved being to be constantly before our eyes.

The Captive—such is the title of one of Proust's volumes, and it is quite true that the dream of certain men (and of certain women) would be to make captives of

233

those they love. Everything that immobilizes the loved being gives them a moment of security. There is an admirable piece in Proust, called *Watching Her Sleep,* in which we see Albertine at last cleansed by sleep of the poisons she contains for Marcel:

"Stretched out from head to foot on my bed, in an attitude whose naturalness could not have been invented, I thought she looked like a long stalk of blooms that might have been placed there, and so it was in fact: the power of dreaming, which I only had in her absence, I regained at these moments in her presence, as though in sleeping she had become a plant. Thereby her sleep realized, in a certain measure, the possibility of love; alone, I could think of her, but she was missing, I did not possess her. With her present, I would speak to her, but I was too absent from myself to be able to think. When she slept I no longer had to talk, I knew that I was no longer looked at by her, I no longer had to live on the surface of my self.

"In shutting her eyes, in losing consciousness, Albertine had shed, one after another, her different characters of humanity that had disappointed me since the day I had met her. She was animated only by the unconscious life of vegetations, of trees, a life more alien to mine, more strange and which yet belonged to me more. Her *self* did not elude me every moment, as when we talked, through the openings of the unavowed thought and the glance. She had called back to herself everything that was outside, she had taken refuge, enclosed, summed up, in her body. In holding her before my eyes, in my hands, I had that impression of possessing her wholly which I did not have when she was awake. Her life was submissive to me, exhaled its light breath toward me.

"I listened to this mysterious murmuring emanation, soft as a sea zephyr, fairy-like as that moonlight which was her sleep. As long as it persisted I could dream of her and yet look at her, and when this sleep became deeper, touch her, embrace her. What I felt then was a love, before something so pure, as immaterial in its sensibility—as mysterious—as though I had been before the inanimate creatures which are the beauties of nature. And in fact as soon as she fell into a somewhat deep sleep she ceased to be merely the plant she had been; her sleep on whose edge I was brooding, with a fresh delight, which I should never have wearied of and which I could have enjoyed indefinitely, was for me a whole landscape. Her sleep placed beside me something as calm, as sensually delightful as those nights of the full moon in the bay of Balbec grown calm as a lake, when the branches barely stir, when, stretched out on the sand,

one could listen endlessly to the breaking of the ebb-
tide . . ."

But if sleep gives respite to the lover, nothing can
wholly cure him, not even death. This immense edifice
which he has built within himself and which is his inner
image of the loved woman, survives the latter, long even
after she has disappeared. When Albertine dies, she
continues to live in Marcel:

"For the death of Albertine to have put an end to my
sufferings, the shock would have had to kill her, not only
in Touraine, but in me, where she had never been more
alive . . . To console myself, it was not one, but innumerable Albertines that I should have had to forget.
No sooner had I disciplined myself to bear the grief of
having lost one of them than I had to begin all over
again with a hundred others."

Ceaselessly his affliction is reborn. The sound of the
elevator evokes the only person whose visit he would have
wished and who would never come again, since she was
dead:

"And in spite of myself, when the elevator stopped on
my floor, my heart would beat, and for a moment I would
say to myself,

" 'What if, after all, it was only a dream . . . Perhaps
it is she . . . She is going to ring . . .'

"All this, however, is not surprising if we consider that

236

even while he or she whom we love is living, a great part of the thoughts that form what we call our love comes to us during the hours when the loved one is not beside us. We form the habit of having an absent being as the object of our revery. And so death does not change a great deal."

This lasts until the moment when finally forgetfulness dissolves the obsessing image. Proust has described at length what he calls *the intermittences of the heart*, that is to say those moments, more and more numerous, when passion, like life at times, stops in us. Since love as Marcel Proust describes it is a mental state, it must some day, like all our mental states, become obsolete, be replaced. Gradually Albertine's image fades, then disappears. At last the moment comes when the image can no longer be revived, save by artistic evocation, and this gives us the admirable episodes of the little *madeleine* cookie or of the rough napkin. But this would take us out of our subject. Let us say only that these images, which seem definitely lost, can be revived, evoked by a perfume, by the sound of a voice, which will awaken for a moment, in the depths of our souls where they slumber, the beings we have loved and who are really dead only the day we have forgotten them.

5. LOVE-AS-COMMUNION

The disease of love, as Proust and Stendhal describe it, certainly exists and their description of the symptoms is accurate. Is it all of love? I do not think so. A scientist can dissect all the organs of a body. He does not in this way reconstruct life. An art critic can describe all the statues, all the stones of a cathedral; he does not thereby give us any idea of the beauty of the cathedral. In the same way, one can conceive a novelist who would admirably describe the mechanism of the passions, and who would miss passion.

Proust speaks somewhere of those gigantic and multiple shadows that are projected on the walls of a dark room by an object on which a bright light is thrown from several directions, shadows which suddenly, if the light floods the place, seem to return to the object itself and to let it finally appear in its reality. In the same way, all the descriptions of the monstrous effects of love leave love itself in the shadow, and the only way to know the latter in its reality is, not through scientific knowledge, but mystic knowledge.

How the artist can attain to the mystic knowledge of the world, how he achieves it by escaping from time, is the whole subject of Proust's great work. Now it seems

238

to me that one could apply to love what Proust has said of art, and affirm that, beyond love-as-disease, there is a mystic love. Imagine that a man and a woman, by the effect of a passionate love, joined to intelligences which passion itself has been able to develop, come to know each other so well that each one can foresee the actions of the other and accept each other's faults; lastly, imagine, what is by no means inconceivable, that the loved object is worthy of the image we have formed of it, or strives to resemble this image, and you will reach a state where jealousy loses all reason for being, where criticism becomes vain, where contemplation suffices for happiness. That this state is rare must be admitted, but that it exists and gives happiness is a fact of experience. Stendhal had an intimation of this in *The Charterhouse of Parma*. Perhaps rather than among novelists we should look for its representation among musicians, and particularly in Mozart. This type of love is lacking in Proust's beautiful descriptions, or more exactly, it has been adumbrated by him only in the form of motherly love.

6. CONCLUSION

There thus exists, beyond the love-as-disease so marvelously described by Proust, a more stable and more complete sentiment, a joy that is not composed only of suffering, a real communion of two beings. But no doubt it was necessary to describe love-as-disease in order to free us from it. The only danger that Proust's minute analysis of the emotions could present was that of creating a generation of analysts, scrutinizing their emotions and destroying them by dint of understanding them too well. Such was, in fact, between the two wars, the weakness of certain disciples of Proust.

But the danger was never very great, nor were the disciples very numerous, because stronger influences worked in a quite opposite direction. We have said that the society observed by Proust was essentially a society of idlers whose members had the time, like the *Précieuses* of long ago, to "de-labyrinth their sentiments". This was no longer the case of their descendants. The war of 1914, by destroying not only fortunes but the stability of all things, from the equilibrium of Europe to the inner constitution of states, had thrown us back toward a type of life which much more resembled the crisis of disorder which coincided with the crumbling of feudal society than a classic civilization like that of the reign of Louis XIV.

Such periods of confusion and anxiety are not propitious to sentiments of too great complexity. These fragile flowers, suited to temperate climates, are choked by more brutal and stronger passions. Religious or political ideas then occupy a large share in everyone's thoughts. Love must become, for harassed creatures, a repose and an appeasement; it must therefore be simple and trusting. In order to die of love like Monsieur de Clèves one must have time on one's hands. An aviator or a sailor, sufficiently absorbed by present and deadly images, is saved from the follies of imagination by the duties of attention.

Undoubtedly there exist innumerable men and women who are accessible to jealousy, to doubt, to passion. Undoubtedly, even, all men and all women remain vulnerable to the "sweet arrows". But they no longer look for the wound; they do not delight in it like Stendhal or Swann; forced in social life to fight, in their emotional life they look for peace and not for war.

Add that the freedom of modern life, the existence in common of the two sexes, on the beaches, in swimming pools, in the snow, engender a comradeship which if not idyllic, is at least healthy and natural, and which tends to bring us closer to love as it was known among the ancients. In many modern novelists—Hemingway, Morand, Jules Romains—one observes in regard to matters of love a cynicism, or more exactly a "naturism", which is much more reminiscent of Greek and Latin literature than that of the French seventeenth century.

In America where until 1918 civilization, except in a few "advanced" groups, had been essentially a chivalrous and Christian civilization where women, as in the Middle Ages, had successfully undertaken to refine the ways of the pioneers, we have witnessed among many young writers since the first world war the rise of a revolt against this feminine vision of life, which had its sweetness, but which threatened to emasculate the men. Against the new romances of chivalry that filled the magazines of large circulation there was to arise a desire for brutality, a craving for obscenity which was a requital. Certain stories of Erskine Caldwell or of Hemingway correspond to what the lusty ribaldry of a Rabelais or a Brantôme were in Europe, at the time of the reaction against the courts of love.

It is curious also to find again, among contemporary novelists, the obsession of death linked to that of love, as in the time of Yseult and of Tristan. For a Steinbeck, for a Malraux, horrors and sexual pleasure are natural companions, and the threat of a violent death adds to the intensity of enjoyment. The old conflicts themselves are recurring. I imagine that there is in the political faith of certain communists a sombre ardor which is reminiscent of that of the martyrs and which, mingled with the passions of love, can for identical reasons produce inner

dramas of the same violence. Thus the history of sentiments, like that of society, turns in a spiral.

Our study has shown that every emotional attitude
after a certain time engenders the contrary attitude. Out
of the extreme and almost inhuman modesty of Madame
de Clèves had come the licentiousness of the Regency;
out of this licentiousness, grown tedious, the virtuous
sensibility of Rousseau; out of the romanticism of the
first half of the nineteenth century, the anti-romantic
novel of Flaubert; out of the Anglo-Saxon puritanism,
the aggressive cynicism whose victories we observe in current American literature. In the same way and for the
same reasons, I imagine that after the cynicism of the
period between the two world wars will follow a new
sentimentality which will be favored, as in the time of
the other Crusades, by absence and by dreams.

So goes the world.